Praise for Holy Jellybeans

"Holy Jellybeans is the perfect title for this beautiful collection of colorful stories and anecdotes combined with God's Word. I love digging through a bag of jellybeans looking for the perfect one. Author Rebecca Carrell doesn't make you dig too far before she says something, a story, a piece of her heart, that touches you and caused you to wonder how you too can impact people in the same way. This is seriously a curl up in your favorite chair with your favorite cup of drink, kind of book. Thank you, Rebecca, for reminding us what it truly means to live out radical and intentional faith."

– Michelle Borquez, President of God Crazy Ministries, Author of *Forever God Crazy, Overcoming the Seven Deadly Emotions, The You Plan,* and producer and host of the *Live Again* DVD series.

"Holy Jellybeans: Finding God through Everyday Things is one of the best devotionals I have ever read. In an honest and transparent way, Rebecca Carrell masterfully takes life stories we can all relate to, and ties them into Scriptural lessons. If you are looking for a book that takes you deeper, *Holy Jellybeans* is an excellent choice!"

– Lisa Burkhardt Worley, former national sports reporter with HBO Sports and the Madison Square Garden Network. Author of *If I Only Had...Wrapping Yourself in God's Truth during Storms of Insecurity* and *Pearls of Promise: A Devotional for Women.*

"Rebecca is one of the most honest and real communicators I've ever been around. Her ability to share spiritual truth through stories from her life - even the messy parts - makes *Holy Jellybeans* a wonderful read! This book will encourage you, that's for sure..."

– Jeff Taylor, ordained minister, morning show host on 90.9 KCBI; former general manager and morning show host of WAY FM network; author of *Life Support: A Prescription for Prolonging the Ministry Life of your Youth Work*

"*Holy Jellybeans* is down-to-earth, inspirational, and delightful--just like Rebecca Carrell. She writes with depth, vulnerability and passion about how God has taught her about His word and His will in the midst of ordinary life. After reading her scripture-filled meditations on simple-yet-profound moments, you'll come away encouraged in your faith and in God's immense, personal love for each one of us."

- Dena Dyer (www.denadyer.com), author of *Grace for the Race: Meditations for Busy Moms*, *Wounded Women of the Bible: Finding Hope When Life Hurts,* and others.

"*Holy Jellybeans* is a soul-filling, calorie-free, delight. Rebecca Carrell has crafted a book that beckons you to read and enjoy the goodness of God. Each page brings points to ponder, quotes to always remember, and sweet satisfaction."

- Lisa Buffaloe (lisabuffaloe.com), host of *Living Joyfully Free* radio, author of *Unfailing Treasures: Finding God's Treasures Along Life's Journey, Nadia's Hope, Prodigal Nights*, and others.

"What a refreshing, Biblically-based, easy-to-digest, relevant book! Such practical lessons that will truly help me be more like Him."

- Janeé Harrell Hill, host of *The Janeé Show* and *R.A.W. – Real Authentic Women*. President of mHe3 Productions (www.mhe3.com).

HOLY
Jellybeans

Finding God through Everyday Things

HOLY
Jellybeans

Finding God through Everyday Things

Rebecca Ashbrook Carrell

Compiled by Anne Hinkle Shannon
Edited by Melissa Fairchild

Clovercroft Publishing

Published by Clovercroft Publishing, Franklin, Tennessee

Published in association with Larry Carpenter of Christian Book Services, LLC, Franklin, Tennessee

Compiled by Anne Hinkle Shannon
Edited by Melissa Fairchild
ISBN 978-1-942557-45-6
Library of Congress Number 2014915344

ACKNOWLEDGMENTS

To Michael James Carrell, the love of my life. I scarcely remember life before you. Thank you for your love, patience, compassion, understanding, and encouragement.

To Caitlyn and Nick, the two most brilliant and beautiful children in the world. God has taught me more through you than you will ever know. I love you beyond my ability to articulate.

To my mom and dad: You have been championing my writing for as long as I can remember. I love you both so much.

To Anne Shannon: Your friendship is one I will cherish forever. Thank you for years of hard work, and thank you in advance for many more years of friendship and ministry. What a privilege it is to serve with you.

To Jeff Taylor, Matt Austin, Joel Burke, and Sharon Geiger: Working with you isn't really work. Thank you so much for the opportunity you've given me at 90.9 KCBI.

To Melissa Fairchild: Thank you, my friend, for your editing skills and your Friendship. I love you.

CONTENTS

INTRODUCTION

As a little girl, I would climb on to my father's lap, snuggle into his chest, and say, "Tell me a story, Daddy!"

My father is a wonderful storyteller. With no preparation or forethought, he would create a magical fantasy world where a princess (who almost always bore my name) and her valiant prince overcame all sorts of evil together.

Today, it's my children who climb on his lap and stare, wide eyed, as my dad spins tale after tale of beautiful princesses and handsome heroes (who are usually named Caitlyn and Nick) in far-off lands.

I think Jesus was a great storyteller too.

If I had been friends with Mary, Martha, and Lazarus, Martha would have found no help in me as she bustled about, preparing for an unexpectedly full house. In all likelihood I, along with Mary, would have sat mesmerized at the feet of our Lord, drinking in every word.

He taught mainly in parables, a short story used to illustrate a moral or religious example. I believe He still teaches in parables, using everyday things and making ordinary objects extraordinary. By His Holy Spirit, He can make the natural supernatural and the mundane miraculous.

He can even do it with jellybeans.

Through my daily walk with Jesus, He has spoken to me through detour signs, a toddler bed, a Jell-O mold, a scraped knee, and, yes, jellybeans.

I invite you to seek Him with me daily. I invite you to allow the Holy Spirit to open your eyes to see how He sees, to teach your heart to love how He loves, and to allow Him to work miracles through you. When Jesus is your ever-present, constant companion, even jellybeans are made holy.

MISSION: WALMART

Six days later Jesus took Peter and the two brothers, James and John, and led them up a high mountain to be alone.

—Matthew 17:1 NLT

Heart pounding and palms sweating, I stood at the end of the checkout lane nervously waiting my turn. A tall, wiry young man with glasses methodically scanned the gentleman's items, carefully placing them into plastic bags.

"Here you go, sir," the young man said, handing the customer his receipt without looking up.

My turn. I took a deep breath, stepped forward, and smiled.

The last time I'd felt this way was in 1992, standing at the starting line of the 3,200 meter race in the regional high school track meet in Denver, Colorado. Now, twenty years later, I felt the same adrenaline rush. Every nerve in my body stood on edge, waiting to fire.

I was about to witness to someone half my age, and I was *terrified*.

The first time I'd laid eyes on Andrew (not his real name) was two weeks prior to W-day (witnessing day). It was a Sunday, and my husband had assumed the after-church-kid-feeding routine so I could grocery shop in peace. I took my time combing the aisles of the local Walmart, carefully comparing prices and weighing options.

I deliberately chose a checkout lane with several people in front of me, so I could flip through the various tabloids I refuse to buy. The line inched forward, and I put *People* magazine down to unload my cart. As I did, I couldn't help overhearing the conversation in front of me.

1

"Ready for your random fact of the day?" chirped the cheery attendant.

"Uh, sure," replied the not-so-cheery customer.

Andrew went on to rattle off a fact that escapes me now but impressed me then. The woman, never making eye contact, simply grabbed her receipt and walked off.

Undaunted, the young man asked me the same question as I approached the register. "Ready for your random fact of the day?"

"You bet!" I responded. Andrew went on to tell me about the world's first computer programmer.

"And," he went on, excitement building, "she was a woman!"

"Wow," I answered, truly impressed. "What else you got?"

"Well," he said, thinking carefully, "did you know that certain types of amphibians can change sex when in a same-sex environment?"

We bantered back and forth for a few minutes. Finally, at what I can only assume was the Holy Spirit's prompting, I asked him, "So tell me: are you an evolutionist or creationist?"

Without missing a beat, he firmly replied, "Evolutionist," and then sheepishly added, "Sorry."

I asked him why he was sorry. He explained his point of view wasn't very popular in Texas, but he was too much of a scientist to entertain anything else.

As I was leaving, I asked him if he'd ever heard of an astrophysicist by the name of Hugh Ross.

"Hugh Ross? Nope."

"I think you'd like him," I said. "Pick up his book *More than a Theory.*" Then, attempting to speak his lingo and earn some cred, I added, "Pay particular attention to the chapter on mitochondrial DNA and the markers left behind when a body, be it virus or animal, evolves or mutates. I think you'll find it fascinating."

"Okay," he responded, eying me with new respect.

"It'll make you think," I said, smiling.

I replayed our conversation again and again over the next few weeks. Praying for him became a daily priority. I asked the Holy Spirit to work on his heart and surround him with Christians, and I solicited my husband and several others to do the same. Somehow, I knew God was doing something with Andrew, and my gut said my assignment was not over.

I was right.

> And He summoned the crowd with His disciples, and said to them, "If anyone wishes to come after Me, he must deny himself, and take up his cross and follow Me. For whoever wishes to save his life will lose it, but whoever loses his life for My sake and the gospel's will save it."
>
> — Mark 8:34–35 NASB

Fast forward to W-Day.

It was a Thursday, and my daughter was with a friend. Nick wanted a playdate too, but no buddies were around, so I promised a day of exciting errands—the bank (free suckers) and Lifeway Christian bookstore (cool toy section).

We made our way into Lifeway, his sucker-coated, sticky hand in mine.

Nick watched Veggie Tales while I browsed the shelves. As far as shopping goes, I struck gold. Bibles were on sale for five bucks each and so was a book called *Evidence for the Resurrection* by author, theologian, and apologist Josh McDowell. I picked up eight books altogether—four Bibles and four copies of *Evidence for the Resurrection*. As I carried them to the register, Andrew's face came to mind.

Take him the books. It started as a whisper, slowly growing louder and louder. I thought of all the very-important-certainly-can't-wait things I had to do. Crucial things, like polish my toenails, shower, and straighten up the house. *I'll keep the books in my car and give them to him the next time I go to Walmart, God. That'll work, right?*

Apparently not.

Two sentences flashed across my brain, completely out of the blue: *Go to Walmart for seeds. Take him the books.*

Seeds? I don't garden. I've got the blackest black thumb there is. But I couldn't shake the notion that I had to go to Walmart for seeds.

3

Besides, I've wrestled with the Holy Spirit enough to know that in the long run, it's easier to obey.

"Come on, Nick," I called out to my son. "We're going to Walmart to get some seeds."

> Your ears will hear a word behind you, 'This is the way,
> walk in it,' whenever you turn to the right or to the left.
>
> —Isaiah 30:21 NASB

Nick and I walked into the megastore, books tucked neatly in my purse. I looked up and down the aisles with an ever-increasing sense of relief. No sign of Andrew. *Sorry God,* I thought. *I'll try again next time.* I immediately heard the still, small voice again, whispering to my soul. *Seeds.*

With a sigh, I walked up to an employee. "Excuse me," I said, smiling brightly. "There is an employee here named Andrew. Do you know if he works today?"

"Andrew?" The man said in surprise, "Yeah, he works today. But not until two o'clock." I looked at my phone—1:22 p.m. "Thank you," I said. "By the way, where are the seeds?"

After killing a half hour looking at toys and bikes, Nick and I made our way to the nursery.

"Okay, Nicky," I said. "What kind of seeds do you think we should buy?" The Holy Spirit had gone silent on the matter, so we decided on bluebonnets, basil, and oregano. Seeds in hand, we walked out to the main store.

My son wanted to jump over every crack on the tiled floor, so I had plenty of time to search the checkout lanes. Finally, at the very last one, we saw Andrew.

I watched him from a distance for a moment. The first time I saw him, he was chipper and upbeat. This time, he met no one's eyes. His shoulders were slumped. He scanned and bagged groceries without looking around or speaking a word. My heart softened as I realized this young man was hurting.

I walked toward the line and waited, seeds in hand. Nick, normally occupied with the candy and toys kept conveniently at four-year-old eye level, stood quietly by my side. The gentleman in front of me took his receipt and left.

My turn.

> Don't worry about how to defend yourself or what to
> say, for the Holy Spirit will teach you at that time what
> needs to be said.
>
> —Luke 12:11b–12 NLT

I cleared my throat. "Got any random facts for me today?" Andrew looked up, eyes wide. He paused before speaking, then said, "Have I told you the one about the very first computer programmer?" He had, but I let him tell me again. We bantered back and forth a bit, then, strength and courage rising, I looked him square in the eye.

"Actually, Andrew," I started, "I came here specifically to see *you* today." The sweet, shocked look on his face nearly broke my heart.

"You did?" he asked, with more than a hint of incredulity.

"Yes, I did," I said firmly. "God has not let me stop thinking about you since I met you a few weeks ago." He set the seeds down and looked right at me. "I know it sounds crazy, but God sent me here specifically today to tell you that He loves you."

Andrew just stared.

"In fact," I continued, "He loves you so much that He has had me praying for you every single day. *Every single day.* And not only that," I said, picking up steam, "He wants you to know that you delight Him. Everything about you delights Him. He wants you to know that He is so pleased with you, and you are exactly the way you are supposed to be."

Andrew was neither blinking nor breathing.

"I know that you're not sure what you believe, and I know you don't know me, but God is bossy, so I have to say this. He loves you so much. He wants you to know that He's real, and He told me to buy you these books."

I handed him a plastic bag with the books. Without taking his eyes off me, he took the bag. "Andrew," I continued, leaning in, "He's real. He's real, and He has a Son, and His name is Jesus, and He so desperately wants you to know Him."

"Um, ok," said the young man, picking up my bag and handing it to me. "Well, thank you."

"You're welcome. Have a great day." And without looking back, I grabbed my son and started walking out of the store.

Once I had Nick buckled in, I opened the bag. As I looked at the seeds, realization swept over me. I had heard God incorrectly. I hadn't gone to Walmart to *buy* seeds.

I'd gone there to sow them.

I bowed my head, thanking God for being so much bigger than I could ever fathom. Thanking Him for allowing me to play a small part in His master plan. I prayed for Andrew, asking God to put mature Christians around him to tend the soil of his heart and to water the seeds I'd planted.

> After six days Jesus took Peter, James, and John and led them up on a high mountain by themselves to be alone. He was transformed in front of them, and His clothes became dazzling—extremely white as no launderer on earth could whiten them.
>
> —Mark 9:2–3 HCSB

Just six days after telling the disciples to take up their crosses and follow Him, Jesus took His inner circle up to the mountain. The gospel of Matthew describes it as a high mountain. What if they had refused to go? What if they had claimed to be too tired or too busy? What if they had stayed back to polish their toes or straighten up their tents?

They would've missed the greatest adventure of their lives.

> And He was transfigured before them; and His face shone like the sun, and His garments became as white as light. And behold, Moses and Elijah appeared to

them, talking with Him. Peter said to Jesus, "Lord, it is good for us to be here; if You wish, I will make three tabernacles here, one for You, and one for Moses, and one for Elijah." While he was still speaking, a bright cloud overshadowed them, and behold, a voice out of the cloud said, "This is My beloved Son, with whom I am well-pleased; listen to Him!" When the disciples heard this, they fell face down to the ground and were terrified.

—Matthew 17: 2–6 NASB

So many of us say we want to follow Jesus. We want the mountaintop experience. But are we willing to climb?

From the bottom of my heart, I urge you to strap on your hiking boots. Make yourself available to Christ. Keep your ear tuned to the Holy Spirit. Pray when He tells you to pray, and speak when He tells you to speak. Go where He tells you to go, no matter how crazy it seems. Whatever you do, don't miss the adventure of knowing Christ. Don't miss the experience of telling someone about the greatest love they'll ever know. Don't miss the hope that flickers in his or her eyes upon hearing of their immeasurable worth.

Please, don't miss the mountaintop.

I have seen Andrew several times since then. I do not know if he has read the books or even glanced at them. But I know I sowed a seed. I pray that others come alongside him to water it and nurture its growth, and that someday I might see him when God calls His faithful home.

Then Jesus said to His disciples, "If anyone wishes to come after Me, he must deny himself, and take up his cross and follow Me."

—Matthew 16:24 NASB

THE SECRET PLACE

Be gracious to me, O God, be gracious to me, for my soul takes refuge in You; and in the shadow of Your wings I will take refuge until destruction passes by.

—Psalm 57:1 NASB

When you were little, did you have a secret hiding place?

I did.

I had a beautiful antique canopy bed that stood about two and one-half feet off the ground. A crisp, white, floor-length dust ruffle encircled it, creating a delightful haven for a young girl.

It was my go-to spot in hide-and-seek. It was a girls-only club with my friends. It was a sanctuary when I was frightened. It was the spot where our cats usually hid, and it was my favorite place to read, play with my dolls, or simply get away.

It was my refuge.

When I outgrew my secret spot, I found another one. This one was outside and only reachable by bike. Our neighborhood sat in close proximity to a wooded park with trails, and I discovered my new hideaway while exploring on my own one day.

There was nothing particularly special or remarkable about it; it was just a little clearing off the beaten path where I would go when I needed to get away. Nothing magical happened there; it wasn't a mystical, spiritual experience. It was just an escape, and somehow, I always came back strengthened.

Do you have a refuge?

He said: The Lord is my rock, my fortress, and my deliverer, my God, my mountain where I seek refuge. My shield, the horn of my salvation, my stronghold, my refuge, and my Savior, You save me from violence.

—2 Samuel 22:2–3 HCSB

Throughout the pages of Scripture, the Lord is called our refuge at least twenty-three times. The concept of a refuge was familiar to the Israelites and important to God. When the Lord spoke to Moses regarding the division of the Promised Land territory, He commanded His servant to establish six cities of refuge for the people. These were cities where those convicted of manslaughter (accidentally killing another) could flee to and receive a fair trial and protection.

TheFreeDictionary.com defines *refuge* as "a place providing protection or shelter" or "a source of help, relief, or comfort in times of trouble." As I've let the notion of God as our refuge roll around in my mind, one thing occurs to me.

A refuge doesn't change your circumstances. Seeking refuge from a storm doesn't stop the rain. Taking refuge amidst a battle doesn't change the war.

It changes *you*.

A refuge allows us room to breathe and space to heal. We're offered rest from that which oppresses us. It allows us to refocus, regroup, and reprioritize. It removes us from the situation for a period of time and offers us a different point of view.

Sometimes in life, we're too close to our circumstances to see them clearly. We need to escape, even if only for a moment.

I have found that when worries weigh me down, there is sweet refuge at my kitchen table. With candles lit, Bible open, and pen in hand, I can bring my concerns to God. I transfer them from my mind to my journal, and as I do, God ministers to me.

Sometimes I get revelations, but usually it's simple reminders.

He reminds me that if He is for me, who could be against me? He reminds me that I am more than a conqueror through Christ. He whispers that my present and temporary troubles are not worth comparing to the glory that will be revealed in me when Jesus comes back, and if I share in His inheritance, I also must share in His suffering.

He reminds me that He loves me, and that if I can trust Him with my pain, He will bring purpose out of it. And then I remember that the one who walked on water, turned water into wine, and calmed the storm is the one who calls me by name and claims me as His.

My circumstances don't change. My perspective does.

And because of that, my circumstances don't look quite so foreboding after all—not when measured against the almighty God.

> God is our refuge and strength, always ready to help in times of trouble. So we will not fear when earthquakes come and the mountains crumble into the sea. Let the oceans roar and foam. Let the mountains tremble as the waters surge!
>
> —Psalm 46: 1–3 NLT

LARYNGITIS

lar·yn·gi·tis:
noun

1. Inflammation of the larynx, typically resulting in huskiness or loss of the voice, harsh breathing, and a painful cough.
   —TheFreeDictionary.com

I hate laryngitis.

I get a nasty case about once a year, and for someone in radio, losing it is the pits.

A typical case for me starts with exhaustion, a difficult state to avoid with a 3:00 a.m. wake-up call. The exhaustion is usually exacerbated by my tendency to overschedule. What can I say? I am determined to find a way to squeeze 26 hours into a 24-hour day.

When I get laryngitis I get the full-meal deal. It starts with a husky voice and doesn't quit until I am completely voiceless, typically for at least three days. Having dealt with this for the better part of my life, I have made some interesting observations:

1. It is easier to discipline my children when I can't talk. It really is. A sharp clap and a stern look quiets them faster than my loudest mommy holler.
2. Other people whisper. This is an amusing by-product of a lost voice, as though my inability to speak affects the sensitivity of my ears.

3. Other people overgesture, and it's hilarious. My swollen vocal cords do not create a need for pantomimed explanations, but I enjoy them regardless.
4. People quiet down and lean in.

The lean-in thing is the most thought provoking. The less volume I have, the harder they listen. They do not interrupt. They watch me intently so as not to miss a word, not because what I have to say is so compelling, though I'd like to think it is. They lean in because they'll miss the words if they don't.

It occurs to me, as I think about this, that God spoke to Elijah in a whisper:

> "Go out and stand before me on the mountain," the Lord told him. And as Elijah stood there, the Lord passed by, and a mighty windstorm hit the mountain. It was such a terrible blast that the rocks were torn loose, but the Lord was not in the wind. After the wind there was an earthquake, but the Lord was not in the earthquake. And after the earthquake there was a fire, but the Lord was not in the fire. And after the fire there was the sound of a gentle whisper.
>
> —1 Kings 19:11–12 NLT

Wouldn't life be easier if God gave us the burning bush? Wouldn't decisions be simpler if He posted road signs at every fork? He can, and He sometimes does, but more often than not, He whispers. That means we have to be still before Him. We bring Him our thanks, our praise, our cares, and our concerns, but if we don't silence our hearts and lean in, we will miss what He has to say.

Hear me as I pray, O Lord. Be merciful and answer me!
My heart has heard you say, "Come and talk with me."
And my heart responds, "Lord, I am coming."

—Psalm 27:7–8 NLT

What was the last thing God said to you? What was the last impression He gently laid on your heart? Do you have a place where His holy reception comes in loud and clear?

I think of all the times when, in my frustration, I cried out for a neon sign, a flashing billboard, or writing in the sky. But if He honored that prayer, would I come to Him more? Would I seek Him in Scripture? Would I try to know His heart? Would I want a relationship with Him?

Would I ever wait for Him in silence?

Our world is a loud, distracting place with dozens of things clamoring for our attention at any given moment. If you want to hear a whisper, you must be intentional and lean in.

God is faithful to hear our prayers and guide our steps anytime we cry out to Him, but the hard work—the *heart* work—happens in the quiet. For me, that looks like my journal, my Bible, and Jesus.

No noise. No interruptions. No cell phones. No Facebook. No kids.

Just Jesus and me. That's where I find peace, joy, and an intimacy with the Creator of the universe that is worth every earthen treasure.

I sought the Lord, and He answered me, and delivered me from all my fears.

—Psalm 34:4 NASB

SPECIAL NEEDS CHILDREN

For He knows what we are made of, remembering that
we are dust.

—Psalm 103:14 HCSB

Early on in my radio career, I had an opportunity to work at the Special
Olympics. That marked the first time I was introduced, firsthand, to
the world of special needs children. Since then, God has given me a
tremendous sense of love and protection for them.

Some time ago, my husband and I attended the funeral of a friend's
mother. It was a sad, somber day. She had fought an illness for years
and left behind a heartbroken husband, a grief-stricken daughter, and
two young grandchildren.

A teenage girl with special needs sat with her mother. Every now
and then the girl shouted out, interrupting the service.

Although her mother was clearly embarrassed, no one gave notice.
There is special grace for those with special needs.

Over the course of the last year, I have been blessed to work with
the special education department of my children's elementary school.
The teachers have endless patience. They persevere with the kids,
encouraging them over and over again. They never get frustrated or
angry. When the children act out, they correct, instruct, and redirect.
They rejoice when the kids succeed at a task and comfort them when
they don't.

If there is one thing I have learned about the special-education
umbrella, it is this: a special need does not give a child permission to
act out or misbehave; rather, it gives them extra grace when they do.

Friend, you and I are God's special needs children.

> I don't really understand myself, for I want to do what
> is right, but I don't do it. Instead, I do what I hate. And I
> know that nothing good lives in me, that is, in my sinful
> nature. I want to do what is right, but I can't. I want to
> do what is good, but I don't. I don't want to do what is
> wrong, but I do it anyway.
>
> —Romans 7:15, 18–19 NLT

I wish I didn't blow it as often as I do, but I'm bent.

So are you.

In fact, all of us are bent toward something. I am bent toward pleasing people.

People pleasers compromise themselves for the approval of others. People pleasers lie, saying things they don't mean to make someone feel good. People pleasers withhold truth under the banner of "sparing feelings." When people pleasers get angry, they often turn into passive-aggressive backstabbers.

People pleasers put the opinions of others over God's opinion.

I have been praying against my people-pleasing tendencies for years, but sometimes I blow it anyway.

In the wake of one particular backslide, I couldn't stop berating myself. I confessed to the party involved, confessed to God, and confessed to people who had nothing to do with the situation. I begged forgiveness from the wronged one and from the Lord. Weeks went by, and I was still under the shame.

One morning, the Lord brought a particular child to mind—a child I love madly and who had a special need.

When the child acts out, I react with special patience and offer special grace. I understand that the child has an underlying condition and, because of this, needs special consideration.

So do you and I.

This grace doesn't give us permission to sin; it gives us grace when we do. It gives us the chance to confess and an opportunity to turn and go a different direction.

God showed me that when I fall into my people-pleaser mode, He sees a young girl who moved every three years growing up. He sees a young girl that had no one to sit with at lunch and no one to talk to in class. He showed me a teenager who wanted so much to be accepted by her peers, and a frightened college freshman, eight hours away from home, desperately trying to make friends.

"Not permission," He whispers, "but grace."

What does He see when he looks at you? What about the coworker you can't stand or the rude person at the grocery store? How about the person in your Sunday school class who nobody likes?

We are each God's special needs child. And when He looks at us, He sees the fractures, scrapes, bruises, and scars we've accumulated over the years. He not only sees our bent nature, but that which bent us in the first place.

And He offers us special grace, and beckons us to do the same.

> But you, O Lord, are a God of compassion and mercy, slow to get angry and filled with unfailing love and faithfulness.

> —Psalm 86:15 NLT

THE FLU SHOT

So you have sorrow now, but I will see you again; then
you will rejoice, and no one can rob you of that joy.

—John 16:22 NLT

I have never been afraid of needles.

Don't get me wrong, I certainly don't enjoy them, but shots have
never bothered me. Maybe it's because I spent my sophomore year of
college donating plasma for cash, or perhaps it's an unusually high
threshold for pain. Whatever the reason, when it's time for the flu shot,
I sign right up.

My daughter takes after me. When she was seven, I took her and
my son to the doctor for a checkup that just so happened to fall at flu-
shot time. She sat there calmly while the nurse cleaned her shoulder
and prepared the needle. I held her hand and told her how brave she
was. When the needle went in, she winced, got the Band-Aid, and that
was that.

Not so for sweet Nick.

My baby is terrified of needles. He is terrified of the doctor's office
because that is where they keep the needles. The mere *mention* of
needles is enough to strike terror into his heart.

I sat there on that cool, clear October day, trying to reason with my
six-year-old.

"Nick, I know you don't want a flu shot, but you need it. The flu is
much, much worse than the shot."

"No, mommy! No, mommy! It hurts! Don't make me get the shot!"

Try as I did, the flu shot is a tough sell. Telling him it was for his own good was no use. Caitlyn, although a wonderful example, was not much help.

"Mommy, you have to tell him the truth. Nicky, it really hurts!"

Thank you, daughter.

When his turn came, I pulled him onto my lap, facing me. I cupped his tear-stained face and kissed his plump cheeks.

"Sweetheart, you have to have a flu shot. Mommy is not going to change her mind. But I am going to hold you as tight as I can, and I promise you I will not let go. I also promise you that this will only hurt for a very little bit."

Surprisingly, it took both the nurse and me to hold his forty-eight-pound body down. Under her instruction, I hugged him as tight as I could to keep him from struggling. His shrieks tore my heart in two.

"Mommy, no! Mommy, no! No! No! Please, mommy, no! Oh-my-gosh-oh-my-gosh-oh-my-gosh!"

Tears welled up in my own eyes as I silently willed the evil nurse to hurry up. When she pulled the needle away, I buried my face in his hair and whispered words of comfort in his ear.

"Okay, honey, all done. That's all. See? No more. I promise, all done. Oh, Nick, I love you so much. I love you so much. It's okay. Everything is fine."

> Dear friends, don't be surprised at the fiery trials you are
> going through, as if something strange were happening
> to you.
>
> —1 Peter 4:12 NLT

How I wish believing in Jesus meant that all our problems disappeared, but that is not the case. The Bible is not a book of stories of wretched people who believed in God, then cruised down Easy Street. On the contrary, the Bible historically accounts faithful people who trumpeted God's glory in the midst of mind-blowing suffering.

My morning show cohost, Jeff Taylor, and I recently had the opportunity to interview pastor and author Max Lucado. I love what he said about suffering:

"People tend to mistakenly interpret the presence of pain as the absence of God. Nothing could be further from the truth."

Who among us has not cried, "Where are you, God?" Who among us has not wondered if our prayers fell on deaf ears? And who among us, in the midst of our darkest valleys, has not secretly questioned our faith?

I have. More than once.

As I sat there, holding my shaking, sobbing son, I wondered how God felt when His Son, His *only* Son, hung dying and bleeding on the cross.

Precious friend, please know that in the midst of your pain and suffering, God is not the nurse with the needle. He is the Father who weeps with you while holding you tightly in His arms. He is the Abba Daddy who whispers words of comfort through the worst of it. He is the Holy One who promises to never leave you nor forsake you. He is the one who sits high above the earth, outside the constraints of time. He is the Alpha and the Omega, the Beginning and the End, the one who spoke the world into being, and the one who knew your name before the world began.

He is the one who causes all things to work together for His glory and your good, and His glory is always good.

And He loves you enough to allow the flu shot.

> I have told you these things so that in Me you may have peace. You will have suffering in this world. Be courageous! I have conquered the world.
>
> —John 16:33 HCSB

KELLEY'S CANCER

For everything there is a season, a time for every activity
under heaven. A time to be born and a time to die. A
time to plant and a time to harvest. A time to kill and
a time to heal. A time to tear down and a time to build
up. A time to cry and a time to laugh. A time to grieve
and a time to dance.

—Ecclesiastes 3:1–4 NLT

I met Kelley Anne McKee in the spring of 1990 at Highlands Ranch
High School in Highlands Ranch, Colorado. Frankly, she terrified me.
My family and I had recently moved from Shoreview, Minnesota, so
there I was, once again, the new kid. At the time, Highlands Ranch was
pretty small. The junior high and high school students met in the same
building, and there had not yet been a graduating class of seniors.

That meant everyone knew the cool crowd.

Kelley was bright, pretty, and popular. She was also a tough-talking,
no-nonsense-taking girl with some of the best double-decker bangs I'd
ever seen. I was instantly intimidated.

I don't remember how we became friends; it just seemed like we
always had been. Ever have a friend like that?

Kelley was everything I wasn't but wanted to be. I couldn't stand
up to anyone; she stood up to everyone. I was timid; she was fearless. I
was self-conscious; she was as confident as they came.

One Friday night early in our junior year, Kelley and I drove into
Denver to go to a dance club called The Mirage. I was driving, and

another car entering the highway cut me off, causing me to swerve into the other lane.

I was also stupid, so I turned on my brights and rode right up on his tail. He slowed down to a crawl, then a stop. I looked at Kelley, wide-eyed and panicking.

"Get out of here," she hollered.

My car chose that moment to stall.

Right there in the middle of the highway, the man got out of his car and banged on my window. I sat there frozen, like a deer in the headlights.

Not Kelley.

She reached over, rolled down the window, and went after the man like a mad pit bull. I was awe-struck, and I knew this chick would be my best friend for a long time.

Long story short, a police officer rolled up and cited the guy. Kelley and I drove off, screaming and laughing hysterically. We weren't angels, but we sure did have one with us that night.

Kelley and I were as tight as could be all through high school. We stayed at each other's houses almost every weekend, and we became part of each other's families.

I remember the sinking feeling in my stomach, waving good-bye as she drove off in her car to K-State. Kelley was the first of us to leave for college, but I took comfort knowing that she'd be only an hour away when I moved my things to KU.

We stayed close throughout college and beyond. Kelley Anne McKee was a soul friend.

> For people and animals share the same fate—both breathe and both must die.
>
> —Ecclesiastes 3:19a NLT

I got the call in 2009. Kelley, now Kelley McKee Kane, was sick, and it was bad. By the time they found the colon cancer, it had reached stage four and had spread to her brain and lungs. I raced up to Kansas to see her.

Kelley was as tough as ever.

Round after round of chemo, and she never complained. Weeks at a time in the hospital did nothing to dampen her feisty spirit. I called her once to comfort her and, in true Kelley style, my friend comforted me.

When my phone rang on October 13, 2013, my stomach sank. It was a Denver area code I didn't recognize.

Courtney's voice broke as she told me that her sister had been moved into hospice with less than a week to live. Two days later, I was on a plane.

God gave Kelley clarity while I was there, and I will cherish those awful, beautiful moments until I see her again in glory. We prayed together. We talked about Jesus, heaven, high school, and kids. I told her I loved her so much, and I would do everything I could to help her two young boys.

I suppose God was merciful when it was time for me to go. Kelley was heavily medicated and sleeping when my sister arrived to take me to the airport. I held her hand and kissed her face. Then I said good-bye for the last time.

I am an inappropriate processor. Nothing hits me when it should. Instead of crying when I hugged her family, I lost it on the plane ride home.

I am also an avoider. I have spent my life running from pain, retreating into books, alcohol, food, exercise, and other people. But at thirty-thousand feet, it was just me, the hurt, and Jesus.

And I had no choice but to press into it. I took comfort in my Savior, who knows just how I felt.

> When Jesus therefore saw her weeping, and the Jews who came with her also weeping, He was deeply moved in spirit and was troubled, and said, "Where have you laid him?" They said to Him, "Lord, come and see." Jesus wept. So the Jews were saying, "See how He loved him!"
>
> —John 11:33–36 NASB

We spend so much time anesthetizing ourselves. We're good at it, and there are plenty of distractions available. But there comes a time when we must surrender to the pain, and when we do, we find that God is faithful.

He is faithful to comfort us when we weep. He is faithful to walk with us through the fire. He is faithful to shelter us in the storm. He is the God of restoration and the God of resurrection. In Him, we have hope, and through Him, we have eternal life. Because of Him, we can say "O death, where is thy sting?" and we never have to say good-bye for good.

As I sat there, sobbing somewhere over Oklahoma, I realized something: to avoid the hurt is to avoid the healer.

I praise You, Father, for a twenty-three-year friendship. I praise You for the beautiful legacy that she leaves behind. I praise You that I will see her again. I praise You that You can help raise her sons. I praise You that she is dancing in glory. Father, I praise You for meeting me in the pain. May Kelley's story comfort others. Amen.

> Then, when our dying bodies have been transformed into bodies that will never die, this Scripture will be fulfilled. "Death is swallowed up in victory. O death, where is your victory? O death, where is your sting?"
>
> —1 Corinthians 15:54–55 NLT

DETOUR SIGNS

This is what the Lord says—your Redeemer, the Holy
One of Israel: "I am the Lord your God, who teaches
you what is best for you, who directs you in the way
you should go."

—Isaiah 48:17 NIV

If you are familiar with the Dallas/Fort Worth area, then you are familiar
with roadwork. I moved to North Texas in 1998, and since then, I cannot
recall a time period without any major construction projects.

Because I leave for work at 4:00 a.m., I miss the morning rush
hour. My thirty-mile commute takes me approximately forty minutes—
unless there's a detour sign.

It used to bother me, but then I started to think about what detour
signs do.

The primary function of the detour sign is to protect. They keep
drivers from hazardous situations and protect construction workers
from careless drivers. As much as I want to race past the detour sign, I
understand that if I do, I could hurt myself or others.

Detour signs slow things down. Unable to take the most direct route,
we are guided along an indirect path. We still get to our destination,
just not as quickly.

Detour signs, if we allow ourselves to view them this way, also
give us the opportunity to see new things. Taking a detour through the
town of Grapevine one day, I discovered several parks and a beautiful
botanical garden. I have lived here for years, but if it weren't for the
detour sign, I never would have known they were there, and I would

have missed hours of free entertainment that a mom with young children is always looking for.

Of course, life is full of detour signs, and most of them have nothing to do with traffic.

> Next Paul and Silas traveled through the area of Phrygia and Galatia, because the Holy Spirit had prevented them from preaching the word in the province of Asia at that time. Then coming to the borders of Mysia, they headed north for the province of Bithynia, but again the Spirit of Jesus did not allow them to go there.
>
> —Acts 16:6–7 NLT

Jesus kept Paul and Silas from Asia. Because of this, the gospel was carried into Europe.

During a major highway construction project, there is an overseer. The overseer knows the whole plan. You and I might know what the ultimate goal is, but we have no way of knowing the details. We have no way of understanding the importance of each step. But the overseer looks at things from a different perspective. As an engineer, he knows exactly when to hold off on something or route things a different way.

God is our overseer. We know the ultimate destination. He knows the details, and if He chooses to slow us down or take us a way that makes no sense to us, we can rest in the knowledge that His vantage point is better than ours.

When I graduated from the University of Kansas in 1996, I had two goals: (1) Get married and (2) Find a job at a country music station morning show. That was God's plan for my life too, but He didn't choose the direct path for me. He placed roadblocks and detour signs in my way. Today, I praise Him for His redirection.

Every time I tried to get my foot in the door of a radio station, I was stonewalled. In all of Topeka and Kansas City, not one program director returned my calls. Swallowing my on-air dreams, I applied for a job that paid sixteen-thousand a year, loading and unloading the promotional van. No luck.

My parents kept asking me to move to Texas to no avail. Discouraged and defeated, I took a job at a plastic surgeon's office that I never should have taken and moved in with a guy that I never should have dated. I shudder to imagine life with him had God not blocked that relationship. After another year's worth of roadblocks, I moved to North Texas.

Doors opened immediately. In four weeks, I had a job at a radio station. In four more weeks, I had a better job at a country station. In six months, I was given the night shift (7:00 p.m. – 11:00 p.m.), and two years later, I was on a country music morning show that just so happened to be the longest-running, most successful country morning show in America. Praise God for holy road blocks!

God's plan is better than your plan. God gives detour signs for a reason. If one way is blocked, it doesn't mean that you're not going to get there, it simply means that you are not going to get there *that* way. Don't make an obstacle out of a detour sign. Remember, detours are often in place to protect you. Do not panic if things seem to be moving too slowly. His timing is always perfect. He is never early or late. Don't get discouraged if His detour leads you into unfamiliar territory. God might have something new that He doesn't want you to miss.

God had something new for me. Six months into the morning show, I met my husband. Five years later, I developed a spiritual itch. Something wasn't right. The job I had fought so hard for was no longer fulfilling. I got back into Bible study, which only made me itchier.

A year later, God called me into ministry only to block every attempt to enter it. Why? The timing wasn't right. I had so much to learn. I had heartbreak to go through. I had brutal pruning to endure. My faith needed stretching and solidifying. I had doubts to resolve and healing to do.

Think of the damage I might have caused if God hadn't blocked my attempts to race out of the shoot like an overzealous bull.

The detours were the best things for me. Compassion sprouted out of the soil of my broken heart. Good fruit blossomed where the pruning took place. Out of my doubts sprang forth a ferocious faith that longs for people to love, know, and grow in Christ.

Our great overseer holds the blueprints to your life. His thoughts are not like ours, and we cannot understand His methods, but we *can* rest in the fact that He loves us. Our hardships are never without purpose. His delays are always divine.

> For You have been my help, and in the shadow of Your wings I sing for joy. My soul clings to You; Your right hand upholds me.

> —Psalm 63:7–8 NASB

UNCUT

God created man in His own image, in the image of
God He created him; male and female He created them.

—Genesis 1:27 NASB

One day, while washing my hands, I noticed my wedding ring was due up
for a good cleaning. The center diamond looked foggy and dull, so I pulled
it off of my finger, plopped it into the jewelry cleaner, and let it sit overnight.

By the next morning, it was a different ring. With the film of grime
washed away, the diamond sparkled as it had the day Mike placed it on
my hand and promised forever. *Much better,* I thought to myself as I
went on my way.

Diamonds are fascinating stones. According to Wikipedia, the word
diamond comes from the ancient Greek word *adámas*, meaning "proper,
unalterable, and unbreakable." The gem is the hardest mineral known
to man, registering a ten on the Mohs scale of mineral hardness. For
thousands of years, the only way to cut and polish a diamond was to
use another one.

When we think of diamonds, we typically picture the flawless gem
adorning most engagement rings. However, there is quite a process
that goes on before the bauble is ready for the jewelry store. The uncut
diamonds are mined either by pipe or alluvial mining. With the former, a
miner harvests around 250 tons of ore to produce a single one-caret stone.

When you find a diamond, the first step is cutting away the matter
encasing it to find the gem. In its uncut state, it looks greasy and grimy;
you might never realize the potential of the stone in your hand. In fact,
raw diamonds lose an average of half their original weight.

Because we have these promises, dear friends, let us cleanse ourselves from everything that can defile our body or spirit. And let us work toward complete holiness because we fear God.

—2 Corinthians 7:1 NLT

Buried deep within the fabric of our soul sits an uncut diamond. We are the crown jewel of God's creation, made in His image. But we're not jewelry-store ready just yet. There is a refining process, and sometimes it hurts.

Like an expert jeweler, God holds each of us tightly, chipping away the unnecessary material and filing off the rough edges. He never takes His eyes off of us. We are always carefully nestled in the light of His love. And when we allow God to work out His perfect plan in our lives, we can rest in the knowledge that all the sifting, pruning, and refining is divinely designed for our ultimate good and His ultimate glory.

Like the faithful Father He is, God does not give up on us. Through trials and storms, He exposes my pride, selfishness, and impulsivity. Bit by bit, He uncovers areas of bondage, not to point out my failures but to restore my freedom.

God challenges each of us to be good stewards of our bodies, finances, and time. He calls us into periods of fasting, silence, prayer, and study. He may urge us to strike up conversations in waiting rooms rather than play on our phones. He calls us to serve when we want to sit. He cuts away our fruitless habits and cultivates our gifts and talents. Why? So we will look less like us and more like His Son.

We know that all things work together for the good of those who love God: those who are called according to His purpose. For those He foreknew He also predestined to be conformed to the image of His Son, so that He would be the firstborn among many brothers.

—Romans 8:28–29 HCSB

You have been chosen. God looks at you and says, "This one is mine." Every storm you go through sharpens you. Each mountain you climb strengthens you. God is refining you, perfecting you, and calling you into a deeper, more intimate relationship with Him. Everything He does has purpose, though we may not recognize it on this side of eternity. He has chosen you to become like His Son, and like a jeweler uses diamond to cut diamond, God uses His Holy Spirit to make you more like Jesus. The final product is brilliant and radiant. It is "unalterable" and "unbreakable," just like the precious stone.

> But we all, with unveiled face, beholding as in a mirror the glory of the Lord, are being transformed into the same image from glory to glory, just as from the Lord, the Spirit.

> —2 Corinthians 3:18 NASB

A STORM, SORT OF

"Yes, come," Jesus said. So Peter went over the side of the boat and walked on the water toward Jesus. But when he saw the strong wind and the waves, he was terrified and began to sink. "Save me, Lord!" he shouted.

—Matthew 14:29–30 NLT

Do you have an outlet? Something you do to release the pressure valve of built-up stress? Writing is my outlet. I have volumes of journals, my earliest dating back to 1987. My mother would tell you I showed a love for paper and pen long before than that.

Having a record of my most secret thoughts spanning almost thirty years is fascinating. First of all, I've learned that I never learn. The mistakes I made in the seventh grade were repeated in eighth, ninth, tenth, and so on. Second, if you didn't know me, you would've thought I was the most miserable person to ever set foot on earthen soil.

I wasn't miserable; it's just that I only journaled when times were tough.

My entries were always letters to God, typically following a predictable formula: "Dear God, here is what I'm worried about. This is what I want You to do about it. I love You. Amen." There were no entries rejoicing over answered prayers and no sweet notes of praise, just a laundry list of holy honey-dos.

Recently, I was thinking about the supernatural life of Peter. He was one of Jesus' three closest companions during His three-and-a-half-year ministry. He had a sideline seat when the transfigured Christ spoke to Moses and Elijah on the mountaintop. He drank wine made from water

31

and ate miraculously multiplied bread. He saw the sick healed and the dead raised to life.

He even walked on water.

Reading this account years ago, I realized that faith keeps us afloat in life's storms.

But what about the good times?

> But that is the time to be careful! Beware that in your plenty you do not forget the LORD your God and disobey His commands, regulations, and decrees that I am giving you today.

> —Deuteronomy 8:11 NLT

I like to imagine the moment Peter stepped out of the boat. The Bible doesn't give us nearly enough details. Was the water squishy and sloshy like a waterbed, or did it feel like stepping into a big puddle? Did he walk up and down over the waves, or did the water supernaturally level out with each step? Did he have to hold out his arms for balance? Was the water cold or warm? What was going through his mind?

Whatever the case may be, we know one thing for certain: while his eyes were firmly locked on Jesus, the impossible was possible. The moment Peter got distracted—the second he allowed his circumstances to become bigger than God—he sank.

I don't have a hard time clinging to Christ when the wind is howling and the waves are crashing. Jesus is the life raft many of us instinctively reach for every time. But when things go our way, we tend to take our eyes off of our Lord. The danger zone, more often than not, lies in the distractions of busyness or monotony. We are more likely to drift when life throws us fame, money, and success.

> For when you have become full and prosperous and have built fine homes to live in, and when your flocks and herds have become very large and your silver and gold have multiplied along with everything else, be careful! Do not become proud at that time and forget

the Lord your God, who rescued you from slavery in
the land of Egypt.

—Deuteronomy 8:12–14 NLT

I don't want just enough Jesus to keep me from sinking, just enough
faith to keep me afloat. I want the sweet consolation of knowing that
He goes before me, walks beside me, and follows behind me. I want the
soft whisper that says, "This is the way; turn around and walk here"
(Isaiah 30:21). I want the adventure! I want to experience peace that
surpasses understanding and wisdom beyond the grasp of men. I want
to live abundantly, love lavishly, and give generously. I want to know
Him like Peter knew Him—through struggles, yes, but also through
sameness, through valleys and victories alike.

Oh, that we would never settle for anything less because, friend, *He
can't get enough of you.*

For God so loved the world, that He gave His only
begotten Son, that whoever believes in Him shall not
perish, but have eternal life. For God did not send the
Son into the world to judge the world, but that the world
might be saved through Him.

—John 3:16–17 NASB

JELL-O MOLD THEOLOGY

But I will rejoice even if I lose my life, pouring it out like a liquid offering to God, just like your faithful service is an offering to God. And I want all of you to share that joy.

—Philippians 2:17 NLT

According to the magazine *Chemical & Engineering News*, Kraft's Jell-O has been "America's Favorite Dessert" for over one hundred years. I can believe that. There is something about Jell-O that makes me happy. Perhaps it's the bright colors. Maybe it's the squishy consistency. Whatever it is, that perfect blend of food dye, sugar, water, glycine, proline, and hydroxyproline makes my mouth water and my taste buds dance.

It's a near-perfect dessert. It's high in chemicals, yes, but it's also low in calories and rich in taste. A dollop of Cool Whip takes it to the next level, and if you really want to up the ante, use a Jell-O mold.

What's better than Jell-O? Jell-O molded into fun shapes!

I was thinking about Jell-O not long ago when I realized that the mold contains far more than semisolidified gelatin; it also contains deep theological truths.

You see, we are the Jell-O, and just like Jell-O, we have been divinely designed to pour ourselves into things. We do it all the time with our kids, our jobs, and our spouses. Some of us pour ourselves into sports or the PTA, committees or HOAs.

I spent many years trying to mold myself into whatever it was others wanted me to be. If I had a dollar for every time I violated my morals to go along with the crowd, I'd never need to work again. I've said things I didn't mean and didn't say things I should have simply because your approval mattered more than my integrity.

There is a problem with that, of course.

After a measure of time, the Jell-O takes the shape of the mold, and it no longer resembles its original form. Sure, you can change its shape, but it involves either a knife or heat (yes, Jell-O melts), and I'm sure neither feels good to the Jell-O.

What is your Jell-O mold? We, like Jell-O, take on a new shape. When you pour yourself into making money, you become greedy. If it's approval you seek, you mirror the crowd. Entitlement often accompanies fame or power, while haughtiness can follow great knowledge.

God has a better mold.

> Therefore, be imitators of God, as dearly loved children. And walk in love, as the Messiah also loved us and gave Himself for us, a sacrificial and fragrant offering to God.
>
> —Ephesians 5:1–2 HCSB

The world's mold is suffocating and constricting. Christ's mold offers freedom from rage, greed, lust, and anxiety. Christ's mold offers freedom from desperately needing approval, from the fear of being found out, from the frantic pace of a life lived trying to keep up with the Joneses.

Forget the Joneses. They're not thinking about you; they're too busy trying to keep up with the Smiths.

Through Christ, the power of the Holy Spirit flows freely, allowing you to live generously, love lavishly, and serve willingly. It is only when we break free from the world's mold that our souls can enjoy the peace that comes from being right with God. Only then can the emptiness in our hearts be filled.

So how does it work?

God's economy is counterintuitive. We are called to turn the other cheek, pray for our enemies, and bless those who curse us. If we are to live victoriously and free from the bondage of sin, we must completely surrender to Christ.

> But whenever someone turns to the Lord, the veil is taken away. For the Lord is the Spirit, and wherever the Spirit of the Lord is, there is freedom. So all of us who have had that veil removed can see and reflect the glory of the Lord. And the Lord—who is the Spirit—makes us more and more like him as we are changed into his glorious image.
>
> — 2 Corinthians 3:16–18 NLT

As we fix our gaze upon our Savior, as we abide in the only source of peace, we take on His characteristics. What are they? According to Galatians 5:22-23, they are love, joy, peace, patience, kindness, goodness, faithfulness, gentleness, and self-control.

Now *that* is a Jell-O mold worth pouring ourselves into.

THE BACKSTAGE PASS

Honor the Lord with your possessions and with the first produce of your entire harvest; then your barns will be completely filled, and your vats will overflow with new wine.

—Proverbs 3:9–19 HCSB

When you work at a radio station, you sometimes get to do fun things.

My career as a DJ has whisked me and my husband off to LA for the Hollywood premiere of the 2004 blockbuster *The Aviator*, where Mike and I met Leonardo DiCaprio, Kate Beckinsale, Martin Scorsese, and Paris Hilton. It's sent us to broadcast live from the ski slopes in Beaver Creek, Colorado. It's taken me to Nashville, New York City, and Las Vegas to watch both the ACM and CMA award shows. I've traded jokes with Blake Shelton and discussed our youths' alcohol problems with Brad Paisley. I've shaken George Straight's hand and given dating advice to Kenny Chesney. I've even sat on stage— yes, *on* the stage— during one of Brooks & Dunn's final concerts.

All of that pales in comparison to the first time I met Taylor Swift. Swift is not a Christian musician, but allow me to make a Christian analogy.

When Taylor Swift comes to town, she comes with a splash. It's not just a concert; it's a major production, complete with costume and set changes between almost every song. You don't watch her sing, you experience full-blown sensory overload in every possible way.

And that's minus the backstage pass.

Visiting an artist backstage is not as exciting as it sounds. You meet at a designated place roughly two hours before the concert begins. You get your pass, a fabric sticker, and you'd better not forget to take it off because if it goes through the laundry, it's there for life (another story for another time).

Either a DJ or a label representative lines you up with about thirty other people and takes you down winding halls with more twists and turns than you can count (by design, no doubt, so you can't sneak back in). Once you get to the room next to the room where you will meet the artist, you stop and wait for approximately twenty to forty-five minutes.

Then the cattle call begins.

The DJ/label representative gives you strict instructions on what you may or may not do (i.e. shake hands but no autographs; get a picture, but not with your own camera; get something signed, but it has to be approved...you get the point), and then they file you through one by one. Then you're ushered back through the endless twists and turns, and that's it.

Unless you're Taylor Swift.

Taylor Swift goes all out. There are no lines, no cattle calls, no strict instructions, no rooms before the room where the artist sits, hidden away from human contact. Instead, you enter a tween girl's wonderland. Gauzy fabric hangs from the ceiling. Soft lamps create an inviting atmosphere where the mouth-watering smell of freshly-baked chocolate chip cookies (yes, made by Taylor) ushers you in and urges you to stay.

Giant barrels of ice boast crisp, refreshing drinks. Pictures from her life and tours plaster the walls. Instead of waiting in line, you lounge on couches. If you don't want to lounge, you can play air hockey, foosball, or video games.

After a short wait, Taylor strides in like she's known you all her life, simultaneously exuding grace and giddiness. Instead of waiting to meet her, she comes to you, graciously thanking you for supporting her music. She doesn't rush through the room, but takes her time, lingering with her guests like the gracious hostess she is, making sure each one feels special.

That's what "all out" looks like. And that's what God does for you.

> We have redemption in Him through His blood, the
> forgiveness of our trespasses, according to the riches of
> His grace that He lavished on us with all wisdom and
> understanding.

—Ephesians 1:7–8 HCSB

God doesn't just accept you; He adopts you as one of His own. He doesn't just make room for you, He builds you a mansion. He doesn't stop at forgiveness; He perfects you, making you holy and blameless in His sight. He deeply desires you. He pursues you daily, without ceasing. He doesn't just offer you grace, He *lavishes* it on you, and He does so with all wisdom and understanding.

Did you need to hear that as much as I did? Let me say it again.

God does not merely allow you to dip your bread in the cup of grace. He invites you to drink, and drink deeply. He showers you with tender mercies with all wisdom and understanding, fully knowing what you've done, what you're doing, and what you will do.

Please don't miss the weight of that. You know the worst thing you've ever done? The one you can't bear to think about? The one you can't forgive yourself for?

He knew you would do it, and He still saved you.

Through His Son, He proves to you over and over again that there are no lengths He will not go to for you.

"Come," He beckons. "Trust me with what you have, and see if I will not open the storehouses of heaven for you!"

Don't give Him a slice; offer up the whole pie and watch Him work. Don't settle for tossing Him a five dollar bill when the collection basket makes its way to your section. Go big. Go all in. Honor Him with your wealth. Give Him the best part of everything your land produces. Give Him your whole life, surrender your whole heart, and watch Him make good on His promises. When you do, you'll discover a delicious truth buried in the gospel of Luke: God is a chronic overgiver.

> Give, and it will be given to you. A good measure,
> pressed down, shaken together and running over, will

be poured into your lap. For the measure you use, it will
be measured to you.

—Luke 6:38 NLT

I don't know about you, but I want the whole thing. I want God's
blessings to spill out all over my lap. I want the whole mess of blessings!

Look back at Proverbs 3. A little grain? No, He will fill your barns
with it. And the (nonalcoholic, for someone like me) wine? God is not
stingy. Your vats will overflow with it. Not boxed wine—the good stuff.

What area of your life have you withheld? Which part of your past
are you clinging to? What stubborn sin is stopping you from enjoying
the rich blessings He has waiting for you?

Let it go. Give Him the backstage pass to your life. Offer Him the
all-access sticker to your heart because, sweet friend, God has gone all
out for you.

Now to Him who is able to do far more abundantly
beyond all that we ask or think, according to the power
that works within us, to Him be the glory in the church
and in Christ Jesus to all generations forever and ever.
Amen.

—Ephesians 3:20–21 NASB

REMODELING

Six days later Jesus took with Him Peter and James and
John his brother, and led them up on a high mountain by
themselves. And He was transfigured before them; and
His face shone like the sun, and His garments became
as white as light.

—Matthew 17:1–2 NASB

Some years ago, I went on a home improvement kick like you've never
seen. I was sitting in my kitchen, loathing the wallpaper. There was a
corner separating from the wall that had bothered me since we moved
in. I fingered the wayward piece thoughtfully and started to pull. In no
time at all, I had about 70% of the paper ripped off.

Mike came home, looked around, and looked at me.

"What's this?" he asked.

"I couldn't stand it for one more second," I replied, "and I want
it off."

That was only the beginning. We had the wallpaper scraped and
the walls textured. We painted as much of our house as we could and
brought in painters to finish the two-story foyer. I meticulously matched
paint to the white baseboards and crawled around on my hands and
knees, filling in the areas where the paint had chipped away.

Before Nick came along, Mike had been using his bedroom as an
office. He'd hung countless pictures on the walls, leaving countless holes
to fill when the time came to turn the room into a nursery. Pregnant and
tired, I opted for covering the holes with a large Cowboys' flag over the
tedious task of fixing them.

The house was exactly the way I wanted it, and then we decided to sell.

I packed up our memories one by one. I prayed over each room, asking the Lord to bless this new family as He'd blessed ours. When I got to Nick's room, I sighed. I couldn't possibly leave the wall in that condition, so I patched up every single one of those holes. The only problem? We had no paint left over to cover them up. So I began the laborious job of trying to match it by making trip after trip to Home Depot and coming back with color cards and sample jars. I couldn't find a blend to save my life. The hours and dollars racked up, but still no luck.

When the new owners moved in, I explained what had happened.

"Don't worry about it," the man said in a slow, southern drawl. "We're pretty much gonna gut the whole house, and I know my wife has already picked out new paint for just about every room."

I stared and gulped. All of my backbreaking work. Friday and Saturday nights painting until one and two o'clock in the morning. Paint on my clothes, my skin, my hair. The money spent on texturing the kitchen walls. The hours at Home Depot. All for nothing.

> Our bodies are buried in brokenness, but they will be raised in glory. They are buried in weakness, but they will be raised in strength.
>
> —1 Corinthians 15:43 NLT

It occurs to me, as I try to find the perfect wrinkle cream under twenty dollars that really does magically erase my crow's feet, how we must look to God as we strive and strain to mold our homes and bodies to fit what society deems as acceptable.

To further illustrate my point, in 2010, the cosmetic and plastic surgery industry raked in over 10.5 billion dollars. Also in 2010, the FDA reported that Americans spent 60 billion on the diet and weight loss industry. These are massive overhauls on bodies that will someday return to dust.

Had Mike and I known that our buyers would gut our house, we wouldn't have spent so much time and effort on remodeling. We would've kept it clean and nice to the best of our abilities, but we could've spent that energy on other things.

> Earthly people are like the earthly man, and heavenly people are like the heavenly man. Just as we are now like the earthly man, we will someday be like the heavenly man.
>
> —1 Corinthians 15:48–49 NLT

Oh, that we could see ourselves from a heavenly perspective: every wrinkle bringing us closer to our glorious body that will never break down. This body will be draped in dazzling white clothes with a face that shines like the sun. Oh, that we could look at ourselves without loathing, remembering that we are fearfully and wonderfully made (Psalm 139:14), seeing gray hair as a crown of glory gained by living a godly life (Proverbs 16:31). Imagine what God could do through us if we remembered that our bodies are His, given to us to steward and use for His glory.

I don't know you. I don't know where you've been or what you're going through. One thing I do know is this: whatever it is will pass. The aches, the pains, the hurt, the heartbreak—while they may be huge now, they are microscopic compared to the landscape of eternity. The Lord of Lords and King of Kings has ransomed you and set you apart for Kingdom things. Your King is coming soon, not for remodeling but resurrection.

> The grass withers and the flowers fade beneath the breath of the Lord. And so it is with people. The grass withers and the flowers fade, but the word of our God stands forever.
>
> —Isaiah 40:7–8 NLT

THE BUTTERFLY

Praise the Lord, who is my rock. He trains my hands for war and gives my fingers skill for battle.

—Psalm 144:1 NLT

With no particular destination in mind, my kids and I were out with the stroller one day. Nick was riding comfortably, and Caitlyn was "helping" me push. All of a sudden, she shrieked and ran about ten feet into a field.

"Mommy! *Butterfly!*"

She was beautiful—brilliant in yellow, black, and white as she flitted through the Texas wildflowers.

Nick and I followed Caitlyn to get a closer look. Our new friend, sensing its admirers, paused nearby, as a queen allowing the commoners to gaze upon her splendor.

"Isn't God amazing?" I asked my children. "He's so creative. Did you know there are over twenty-thousand species of butterflies in the world?" Caitlyn and Nick stared at me blankly for a moment before running off in search of more.

Their efforts proving fruitless, we moved on.

Later that night, as I got ready for bed, I turned on a Christian talk radio station. The pastor was telling a story about a butterfly, and I want to share it with you:

A man was working in his yard one day when he came across what he believed to be a cocoon. He looked at it in fascination, then went on with his work.

Over the course of the next few days, he would check back on it periodically, hoping to see the new creature emerge. Finally, he noticed a small hole. As he watched, the butterfly began to slowly work its way out of the cocoon.

After a few minutes, it stopped. The man waited about fifteen minutes, then, concerned for the butterfly, went inside to fetch a tiny pair of nail scissors. With a surgeon's precision, he snipped a line in the cocoon and gently pulled it apart.

The butterfly emerged with a swollen body and shriveled wings. What the man did not know was this: God designed both the butterfly and the cocoon with a purpose. As a butterfly pushes and struggles against the walls of the cocoon, fluid is pushed out of its body and into its wings. The butterfly is strengthened through the adversity. It is only after it works its way out that it is strong enough to survive in the outside world. With only the best of intentions, the man had robbed the butterfly of its chance to survive and thrive. It died shortly after.

As a runner, I have to push myself out of my comfort zone every day in order to go faster and farther. It's only when my legs are crying out in pain that I gain strength and endurance. A body builder consistently seeks to challenge his muscles by increasing the weight. He drives himself to a place where his muscles shake and sweat pours down his face. Then he knows he is adding mass to his body.

Why do we fear trials so much? If you are anything like me, you prefer the safety of sameness to the chaos of change. A place for everything and everything in its place, and when something is moved, we fall apart.

Notice the way King David describes God in Psalm 144:2 in the HCSB: "He is my faithful love and my fortress, my stronghold and my deliver. He is my shield and I take refuge in Him; He subdues my people under me." David displayed the kind of trust and confidence in the Lord that comes only through weathering some storms. Each time, God saw him safely through. Nations had come against David, and God subdued them while he watched.

Spiritual growth comes from seeking and trusting in God. We're strengthened as we climb the hills and fight our way through the wilderness. Anyone can praise Him in the sun, but can we praise the Son in the wind and rain?

It occurs to me, as I reflect on my journey and the dark valleys He has carried me through, that had I not endured the hardships, I would not have a ministry. Storms have a way of sharpening our focus and reshaping our priorities. You would not be who you are had you not gone where you've been.

What if we viewed challenges and valleys as opportunities to watch God work? What if we asked Him to strengthen us *through* instead of deliver us *from*? God faithfully keeps His promises, but His time line may be different than yours. If you are going through a storm, know this: He is with you. He will comfort you. He will never forsake you. He is strengthening you. It will pass. And you will see beauty on the other side of the pain.

HOARDERS

Don't store up treasures here on earth, where moths eat them and rust destroys them, and where thieves break in and steal.

—Matthew 6:19 NLT

It takes seven seconds for me to get sucked into a reality show. Pick a show—any show. No matter how bad it is, if I watch it for seven seconds, I'm hooked.

Fortunately, my schedule doesn't allow me to sit around and watch very often, but every now and then, I find myself standing in front of the TV, remote control in hand, eyes wide and head shaking at what people are willing to reveal on television.

My most recent mouth-gaping, head-shaking experience? *Hoarders*.

If you haven't watched in horror along with me, *Hoarders* spotlights people with a legitimate mental disorder. In a nutshell, they can't throw things away.

The episode I watched involved an elderly woman and food. Her freezers, bursting at the seams, were duct-taped shut. She had two refrigerators (not uncommon) stuffed to the gills with rotting yogurt, cottage cheese, and every kind of perishable item you could imagine (highly uncommon). When her fridges could hold no more, she would stack fruit and vegetables anywhere she could find a square inch.

When the team arrived to assist with the clean out, she refused to part with yogurt that was seven months past its expiration date, claiming that if it wasn't "stinky or swollen," it was still edible. The crew removed liquefied bags of carrots, maggot-ridden cuts of meat, and cartons of cracked and rotting eggs.

The most eye-opening moment came when the team (wearing hazmat masks) tried to remove (by shovel) a partially liquefied squash, and she wouldn't allow it until she had picked out the seeds.

Her environment was toxic, and she was a prisoner in it.

How many of us, in a spiritual sense, live the same way? How many of us need the storage rooms of our hearts and minds cleaned out?

> Casting all your care on Him, because He cares about you.
>
> —1 Peter 5:7 HCSB

The human heart has a tendency to hoard.

We hoard bitterness, resentment, unforgiveness, and jealousy. Some of us hoard grief. Others cling to past accolades and achievements, while still others keep a white-knuckled grip on their failures, unable to step out in faith for fear of repeating old mistakes.

Some of us hoard schedules, clenching calendars in one fist and car keys in another, always scurrying from one thing to the next, never enjoying where we are and never leaving room for the Holy Spirit's guidance. Kids become a casualty, along for the stress-filled ride.

What are you clinging to?

I have a history of hoarding approval. I've said things I shouldn't have so people would listen to me. I've sat by silently so people wouldn't get mad at me. I've spent years filling my calendar with a never-ending stream of activities because I couldn't say no, clinging to everything but Christ for security.

> Cast your burden upon the Lord and He will sustain you; He will never allow the righteous to be shaken.
>
> —Psalm 55:22 NASB

I couldn't experience contentment until I allowed the Holy Spirit to come in and clean out my heart. It was quite a job.

With His holy hazmat mask, He cleared out resentment from past relationships and disappointment from dreams not fulfilled. He washed away fears of the future and shame from mistakes.

As I trusted Him with my heart, He healed it.

What are you hoarding?

You can let go.

You can set your burdens down. You can surrender. You can let go of your fear and trust Him with your future.

You can release those who've failed you. He will meet you in the pain you persistently suppress.

He will fill the empty places inside you. He brings with Him peace, joy, and contentment.

> And I will make an everlasting covenant with them: I will never stop doing good for them. I will put a desire in their hearts to worship me, and they will never leave me. I will find joy doing good for them and will faithfully and wholeheartedly replant them in this land.
>
> —Jeremiah 32:40–41 NLT

THE FISH

And many will turn away from me and betray and hate each other. And many false prophets will appear and will deceive many people. Sin will be rampant everywhere, and the love of many will grow cold.

—Matthew 24:10–12 NLT

If you ever need an example of our Divine Designer's imagination, might I suggest the Grapevine Mills Mall Aquarium in Grapevine, Texas?

On a whim one day, I took my son. We made our way slowly through an underwater wonderland filled with fish of every shape, size, and color—sharks, giant stingrays, sea turtles, and sea horses.

If you visit, take your time in the first room. You might see our fish.

The first room is encased by a circular aquarium. As you stand in the middle, looking about, the fish swim around and around, propelled forward by a man-made current—never stopping, just swimming in circles.

I was tired the day we went. I was also unimpressed with hundreds of fish swimming in the same direction, so I leaned against the wall and waited for Nick to get bored.

Lulled by the monotony, my thoughts wandered as my eyes glazed over. I shifted, sighed, and glanced at my son. He seemed riveted.

Curious, I looked up to see what had captured his attention, and there he was: a rebel, perhaps the James Dean of the bunch—one lonely fish swimming against the crowd.

Nick and I watched for at least five full minutes. Down dove the fish, and then back up, straining against the flow of the water. The other fish paid him no mind, swimming to his right or his left, intent on staying the course. I found myself rooting for him, silently applauding his individuality.

Eventually, the effort proved too much or the current proved too strong, and our new friend gave up and fell in line with the others. Nick and I moved on to the next exhibit.

I thought about the incident all day—our upstream fish in a downstream world. It occurs to me that as strong as his current was, the current we fight is stronger.

> Enter through the narrow gate. For wide is the gate and broad is the road that leads to destruction, and many enter through it. But small is the gate and narrow the road that leads to life, and only a few find it.
>
> —Matthew 7:13–14 NIV

Perhaps no one has a greater fight than the godly man. We live in a sex-saturated society that denigrates women to objects designed for the sole purpose of bringing pleasure. Not long ago, I stood in the checkout lane, silently thanking God that my daughter—who reads beyond her grade level and was the perfect height to see the cover of "The Sex Edition" of *Cosmopolitan*—chose instead to play with the trinkets and toys on the other side of the aisle. A frustrated friend recounted a shopping trip with her six-year-old daughter. Looking for summer clothes, she left empty-handed after finding nothing but shorty-shorts in several department stores. My husband, an avid weight lifter, subscribes to a fitness magazine to get ideas and tips for a more effective workout. Peppered in between the articles are full-page ads promising to "get her in the mood" and to "give you maximum endurance…in the gym and in the bedroom." One full-blown ad showed two scantily clad, erotically positioned women in bed. The "article" that followed promoted a step-by-step video instruction guide, presumably given by the women, on how to please your girl.

Men aren't the only ones swimming upstream in this area. A popular book series, celebrated by fans as "mommy porn," sat on *The New York Times* best sellers list so long that *Time* magazine ran a front page headline when it fell off.

Once upon a time, if you wanted to view inappropriate material, you had to leave your house and risk being seen in a theater or adult store. Today, it follows you via pop-up Web sites or e-mail marketing. Adult content is predatory, stalking our men and children. In 2012, the average age a child viewed pornographic material was ten and usually by accident on their home computer.

Although the hypersexualization of our world may be the most obvious issue, it's not the only one we work against. Society sees no problem with weaning two-year-olds off the binky, only to pacify them with TV, DVDs, and video games. The American Academy of Pediatrics says no screen time (which includes TV, movies, cell phones, and tablet computers) for children under the age of two, but the average infant to toddler is exposed to two hours a day. American culture tells us that our children, preadolescents, and teens need sports and activities around the clock if they're ever to make anything of themselves. Heaven forbid they have time enough to be *bored* enough to imagine or create.

A prime-time news network recently reported that one-third of today's youth is overweight. It is scarcely surprising when restaurant portions contain enough calories for one day, and you can feed a family of five at a fast-food joint for the price of the ingredients to make a salad. In order to maintain health and fitness in a world where the affordable food is processed, sugar-filled, and tailor-made to create food addictions, you have to swim upstream.

Minority groups are pressuring the government to redefine institutions that date back to the creation of man and strong-arming our churches to reinterpret the Bible that defends these institutions.

And the Bible says, if I might paraphrase, expect choppy waters.

> For a time is coming when people will no longer listen
> to sound and wholesome teaching. They will follow
> their own desires and will look for teachers who will

tell them whatever their itching ears want to hear. They
will reject the truth and chase after myths.

—2 Timothy 4:3–4 NLT

To be a loyal follower of Christ today means that you'll sometimes
feel like the fish—the only one swimming north in a southbound stream.
You will feel like the lonely voice of reason in the midst of depravity.

Fight the current. Do not get discouraged. Swim on. Be intentional,
even radical. Remember the words of Jesus:

> God blesses you when people mock you and persecute
> you and lie about you and say all sorts of evil things
> against you because you are my followers. Be happy
> about it! Be very glad! For a great reward awaits you
> in heaven. And remember, the ancient prophets were
> persecuted in the same way.

—Matthew 5:11–12 NLT

Swim on, friend, and know that you are not swimming alone.

STARBURST JELLYBEANS

"But forget all that— it is nothing compared to what I am going to do. For I am about to do something new."

—Isaiah 43: 18–19a NLT

When you have your first child, you will hear one saying over and over again: "Remember these days. They really do fly by!"

Outwardly, I would nod enthusiastically and agree, while inwardly I'd roll my eyes. The years might fly, but the minutes felt like years.

Today, I find myself giving that same advice. How is it that we're done with cribs? We've said good-by to binkies, blankies, and diapers once and for all. How is it that, after five years, I no longer have a child in preschool?

One morning, I was late dropping the kiddos off at said preschool. I breathlessly herded my daughter into the building and impatiently waited for my son to make his way to the door. Once Nick was squared away, I hustled Caitlyn to her classroom.

"Sorry I'm late!" I said, as I signed my daughter in. "No problem," smiled the teacher. "Did you bring your Easter items?"

Like a deer caught in the headlights, I stared back at her.

"The eggs," she prompted. "You had signed up to bring eight plastic eggs filled with Starburst jellybeans."

"Right," I said. "Of course. I'll be back in twenty minutes."

"You can turn them in at the end of class," she replied sweetly, then reiterated, "Eight eggs with *Starburst* jellybeans."

"Got it!" I replied, dashing toward the door.

Berating my forgetfulness, I buckled in and started the car.

Okay, I debated silently. *Walmart or Target?* Since I knew exactly where the Easter display was, I chose Walmart.

I parked my car and strode purposefully into the store—a woman on a mission. I grabbed a cart, headed toward the candy, and started to search.

"Starburst jellybeans, Starburst jellybeans, wherefore art thou, Starburst jellybeans?" I said to myself.

They had Jolly Rancher jellybeans, Braches jellybeans, and Jelly-Belly jellybeans. There were chocolate bunnies galore as well as peeps of every shape and size. It looked as though I had entered into the Easter Bunny's secret vault; every single kind of candy under the sun *except* Starburst jellybeans.

I sighed. "Just my luck," I said to myself. I had a mile-long list of things to do and only three short hours to do it. Since I was already there and the prices were cheap, I started picking out Easter items for my kids. I found the plastic eggs and made my way toward the cashier. I stopped, scouring the jellybeans once more.

"They will never know if you don't use Starburst jellybeans," whispered a little voice. "You really think they're going to pop those eggs open and look to see if they've got the 'Starburst' stamp on them?" I slowly reached toward the Jolly Rancher jellybeans. And then I heard it loud and clear—the teacher's cheery voice, chirping, "Eight eggs with *Starburst* jellybeans!"

I paid for my things and loaded my car. "Okay, Lord," I said out loud. "Clearly there is something you want me to see or do at Target. Let's go."

After a few tense moments of fruitless searching, I found what I was looking for. I paid for my Starburst jellybeans and went back home to stuff the eggs.

Focus on the Family was on the radio. The host was interviewing a man with a southern drawl and who was talking about fear. "You know," he said, "in all my research, I've found mankind's biggest fear is the fear of being insignificant. It's the fear of not mattering. We all want to be taken seriously. We all want to leave some kind of mark when we go." I turned up the radio and leaned in.

The speaker continued, "If we want to really outlive our life, we need to trust God will open the doors. And," he said, pausing for emphasis, "we need to trust Him when He *closes doors*. I had a hard time with that." He went on to explain that he'd felt God telling him to step down as senior pastor of his church in San Antonio, a decision he struggled with.

Eventually, the host addressed the speaker by name. The guest was one of my favorite authors, Max Lucado, and I realized that God had orchestrated my entire morning so that I would hear those words: "We need to trust Him when He closes doors."

In the story of Sodom and Gomorrah, two angels arrived at Sodom to remove Abraham's nephew from the city before the Lord destroyed it. But Lot's wife had lived there all her life, and despite the angels' firm instructions to run and not look back, she hesitated.

> Then the Lord rained down fire and burning sulfur from the sky on Sodom and Gomorrah. He utterly destroyed them, along with the other cities and villages of the plain, wiping out all the people and every bit of vegetation. But Lot's wife looked back as she was following behind him, and she turned into a pillar of salt.
>
> —Genesis 19:26 NLT

I had been struggling a bit, clinging to something God wanted me to let go of. It was something that made me feel relevant and gave me a sense of identity. He wanted me to surrender my part-time status at the country music radio station that I had left.

I have a passion, a fire in me, to encourage women to find their identity in Christ, to let go of the world's definition of success and beauty, and to see themselves through the eyes of Jesus. I want to share my story, where I've been, and what He has delivered me from. I want them to know that if God can deliver me, if God can give me a clean heart and clean hands, and if God can redeem me, then He can most certainly deliver you.

God was telling me to turn a page, let go, and follow Him with an undivided heart and mind. He was telling me that my obedience was the only necessary ingredient in the equation.

We cannot move forward when we are looking back. Once during a high school track meet, I broke a cardinal rule: I glanced back to see where my competition was. That look did two things: (1) slowed me down and (2) steered me off course. I bumped into another runner and promptly toppled over, losing even more time. After I crossed the finish line (third from last), my coach let me have it.

"Don't ever look back," he scolded. "Don't check your progress, and don't worry about their race. Just run forward hard!"

And God used Starburst jellybeans to remind me of that. If it weren't for the jellybeans, I wouldn't have heard what God had to tell me that day. I might not have left that job, and I would have missed the blessings of obedience.

> "Look! I am creating new heavens and a new earth, and no one will even think about the old ones anymore."
>
> —Isaiah 65:17 NLT

THE SOCCER GAME

Finally, be strong in the Lord and in the strength of His might. Put on the full armor of God, so that you will be able to stand firm against the schemes of the Devil.

—Ephesians 6:10–11 NASB

For a brief period in the spring of 2010, I officially bore the title of "soccer mom." I didn't have a minivan, but I was a soccer mom nonetheless.

My husband and I signed our daughter up for Upward through our church. Upward Sports is a Christian ministry emphasizing good sportsmanship and teamwork above competition. Every child gets to play, regardless of skill or experience. The teams don't keep score, which is good because over the course of the season, our team (the Rainbows) put the ball in the goal twice.

My husband, who thrives in a competitive atmosphere, decided that until our daughter garnered more skill, her best bet was to play defensively. He would race her around the backyard, hollering, "Kick the ball away, Caitlyn! Kick it away!" and "Get in front of that goal, honey! That's right!"

At one of her games, Mike and I were pleased to see his efforts pay off. More than once, Caitlyn managed to maneuver the ball away just as the other team prepared to score (again).

Defensive tactics are helpful, but they won't win the game. If you want the win, you must put the ball in the opponent's goal.

I smile as I remember the first time I pulled Caitlyn's tiny pink shin guards over her skinny little legs. I recall wishing that she would wear them every day, soccer or not. Her shins and knees bore the battle scars of an active childhood. Shaking my head, I laughed, thinking of how ridiculous she would look wearing pink shin guards to school. In a game, however, you can't play without them. A swift kick from a cleated foot could fracture or break your tibia, knocking you out of the game or even the season.

For an athlete to be effective, she must suit up appropriately. For a Christian to gain ground, she must do the same.

> Stand your ground, putting on the belt of truth and the body armor of God's righteousness.
>
> —Ephesians 6:14 NLT

What is the sturdy belt of truth? In John 14:6, Jesus told disciples, "I am the way, the truth, and the life. No one can come to the Father except through me" (NLT). Society says that there are many ways to God, many ways to win the game. This is not so. You can be the fastest runner on the field. You can have the best moves and the fanciest footwork, but if your coach isn't Christ, you are scoring points for the opposing team.

> For shoes, put on the peace that comes from the Good News, so that you will be fully prepared.
>
> —Ephesians 6:15 NLT

Watching the little girls play their first game was so cute. We'd had all of two practices, and none of them came with game-day experience. More than anything else, it was their nerves that hindered them. The wide-eyed four-year-olds stood frozen, overwhelmed by the sounds of whistles blowing and parents screaming.

The coach pulled them over to the side.

"Girls, we can do this! It doesn't matter if you make a mistake. Try your best, play your hardest, and have some fun!"

I wish I'd had a sideline seat when Jesus called His followers into the huddle and laid out His game plan. I imagine Him leaning in, meeting each of their eyes as He explained how He would leave them for a time and how they would scatter and grieve while the world rejoiced.

How did the disciples feel when the One they'd sacrificed everything for and banked everything on told them He was leaving the game?

"I have told you all this so that you may have peace in me," He said (John 16:33a NLT).

Peace? Jesus is leaving them, and they should feel *peaceful* about that?

"Here on earth you will have many trials and sorrows." And then, the trick play, the ace up His holy sleeve: "But take heart, because I have overcome the world" (John 16:33 NLT).

The beauty of Upward is this: the kids are free to play their hearts out, have fun, and make mistakes because they don't keep score. It's not about winning, it's about playing. It's about camaraderie and teamwork.

If you walk with Christ, you walk in victory. You are free to play, try, and make mistakes, provided you get back up. You are not defined by your fouls, your fumbles, or your failures. No matter how discouraged or defeated you feel, the fact is that you are on the winning team. Therefore, it is no longer about winning. We've won. It's about running with endurance and playing hard. It's how we live and how many lives we touch. It's about sharing our story and sharing the good news. It's about loving extravagantly, serving sacrificially, and giving generously. Finally, it's about shining His light in a steadily darkening world.

We will lose a battle here and there, but the war, sweet friend, is won.

> They conquered him by the blood of the Lamb and by the word of their testimony, for they did not love their lives in the face of death.
>
> —Revelation 12:11 HCSB

COUNTERINTUITIVE

Then one of the twenty-four elders asked me, "Who are these who are clothed in white? Where did they come from?" And I said to him, "Sir, you are the one who knows." Then he said to me, "These are the ones who died in the great tribulation. They have washed their robes in the blood of the Lamb and made them white."

—Revelation 7:13–14 NLT

Have you ever fallen in love with a word?

My grandfather, William Sinclair Ashbrook, Jr., was an extraordinary wordsmith. He had a beautiful, expansive vocabulary. A conversation with Poppa typically sent me searching for a dictionary, and I often wondered if he kept a pocket thesaurus stashed in his coat.

Nonna and Poppa made it a point to visit us once a year. Imagine it: three kids, a cat, a yippy dog, and grandparents who weren't used to noise. Poppa sat parked in my father's chair, brandy in one hand and a cigarette in the other. "Goodness!" he exclaimed as my sisters and I bickered. "What a monstrous cacophony!" I had never heard of a *cacophony*, but I loved the sound of it and made a note to look it up.

Cacophony – Jarring, discordant sound; dissonance (thefreedictionary.com)

Poppa and I shared a love of words.

My love of words also trickled into other parts of my life. For seven years, I sang on our church's praise team. Excluding me, it's a talented group of seasoned, professional musicians. The electric guitar player, Jack Balderson, who masquerades as an attorney by day, was helping me work out a tough harmony. I said something to the tune of, "Why can't I get this?" He responded, "Well, it's very counterintuitive." My simple mind latched onto the word, tucking it away for future use.

Counterintuitive – Contrary to what intuition or common sense would indicate (thefreedictionary.com).

Everything about Jesus is counterintuitive. Remember the Sermon on the Mount? According to our Savior, we are blessed when we are poor in spirit, meek, and persecuted. If someone needs a shirt, offer them your coat as well. If someone strikes your right cheek, don't hit back. Instead, let them hit your left cheek, too.

> So Jesus called them together and said, "You know that the rulers in this world lord it over their people, and officials flaunt their authority over those under them. But among you it will be different. Whoever wants to be a leader among you must be your servant, and whoever wants to be first among you must be the slave of everyone else."
>
> —Mark 10:42–44 NLT

What does our behavior say about us? Do we belong to Jesus or the world?

Once, rushed to get dinner started, I ran to the grocery store for a handful of items. Spotting an empty lane, I strode toward it, grateful for an in-and-out trip. Another woman, who had a full cart, sped up to beat me to it. Disbelief turned to anger before I remembered Jesus' words: "But among you it will be different." As counterintuitive as it is, we are called to be last.

It happens every day in parking lots, on highways, and at the office. Working in radio requires a willingness to open oneself up to scrutiny. When angry listeners shoot off fiery e-mails, it hurts, and my first reaction is to fire one back. But Jesus, in His counterintuitive way, tells us to bless those who curse us and pray for those who persecute us, which is admittedly difficult in a society that puts self above all else.

The world hoards money, giving only out of abundance, while Scripture commands us to give our first and best fruits.

> What sorrow awaits you who are rich, for you have your only happiness now. What sorrow awaits you who are fat and prosperous now, for a time of awful hunger awaits you. What sorrow awaits you who laugh now, for your laughing will turn to mourning and sorrow. What sorrow awaits you who are praised by the crowds, for their ancestors also praised false prophets.
>
> —Luke 6:24–26 NLT

Jesus wasn't condemning the wealthy. Christ's warning is for those who put wealth above all else and trade integrity for praise. He is condemning those who are more concerned with *who* they are than *whose* they are. These are all issues I struggled with as I built up the courage to leave a successful career that paid well for a ministry that promised nothing.

> Then He said to them all, "If anyone wants to come with Me, he must deny himself, take up his cross daily, and follow Me. For whoever wants to save his life will lose it, but whoever loses his life because of Me will save it."
>
> —Luke 9:23–24 HCSB

Everything about Jesus is counterintuitive. Two-thousand plus years ago, He turned the world upside down and turned His small band of believers inside out. Those who are last shall be first. Those who die to self shall live. Those who humbly serve will be lifted up. Go the extra mile. Consider your trials pure joy. These are the commands Jesus gives.

Yes, He is counterintuitive. Nothing about Him makes sense, but it was His unfathomable love, His immeasurable grace, and His unsurpassed mercy that won you over in the first place.

Pass it on. Be Jesus to those who hurt you. Live counterintuitively, and you will watch Him work in you, on you, around you, and through you.

May I leave you with one final word? It's drenched in richness and promise, and is the essence of His love and provision toward you: *abundantly.*

> Now to Him who is able to do far more abundantly beyond all that we ask or think, according to the power that works within us, to Him be the glory in the church and in Christ Jesus to all generations forever and ever. Amen.
>
> —Ephesians 3:20–21 NASB

THE UNDERTOW

So we must listen very carefully to the truth we have heard, or we may drift away from it.

—He;brews 2:1 NLT

It was the hot, dry summer of 2010 when my family (both immediate and extended) took a beach vacation to Ocean City, Maryland. My grandfather had passed away a few months before, and he'd requested that we scatter his remains in the bay. Poppa lived an extraordinary life, spending the last two decades traveling the world via cruise ship. He was a university professor, published author, and opera lover who fluently spoke at least five different languages. His irresistible charm had won the hearts of countless caregivers in his final days, and when he passed, he was sorely missed. Everyone who knew William Sinclair Ashbrook, Jr. loved him. So while the loss stung, it was with full hearts that we said our final good-byes.

Our family is widely scattered across the United States, so we made the most of our time together, eating fresh seafood each night and playing on the beach by day. It had been years since I swam in the ocean, and I was eager to feel the sand between my toes and smell the salty air. I took Caitlyn by the hand and we ran together, full speed, toward the frothy surf.

We were no more than a few yards in when my four-year-old slipped and got swept along in the undertow. I had forgotten the strength of the ocean current. I quickly picked my daughter up and, having been frightened by her fall, Caitlyn ran toward the beach.

A beach trip with small children (ten between us) is a lot like playing defense: blocking one child from pouring sand on a cousin's head, chasing a toddler down the shore, pulling a three-year-old out of another family's Cheetos, and so on and so forth. One afternoon, Mike, sensing I needed a break, offered to take the kids to the pool for a bit. I thought about sneaking back for a quick nap, looked at the crashing waves, and made up my mind.

I dove into the surf and swam for the better part of an hour. Calling it a day, I worked my way toward the shore and collapsed on the sand. I lay there a moment, enjoying the rare time to myself. In the distance, I could faintly hear the familiar tune of a country song as children laughed and squealed. I got up, stretched, and looked around. Confused, I blinked my eyes and looked again. I didn't recognize a single thing. The undertow had pulled me roughly one hundred yards from my starting point!

> Don't copy the behavior and customs of this world, but let God transform you into a new person by changing the way you think. Then you will learn to know God's will for you, which is good and pleasing and perfect.
>
> —Romans 12:2 NLT

The pull of the world is every bit as strong as the ocean's undertow. In Ocean City, I learned that if I am not swimming against the current, I am being pulled along with it. Likewise, if we aren't actively seeking Christ, we are drifting away from Him. I've done it more times than I care to count; storms will spring up and I'll cling to Jesus with all my strength. Things calm down, and I loosen my grip.

It's frightening how easy it is to drift. It takes no effort on our part. If you want to stay in the same spot in a body of water, you've got to anchor yourself. Otherwise, you're at the other side before you know it. You cannot drift upstream, and our world is flowing downstream at an ever-increasing rate. In his second letter, Peter writes, "I am warning you ahead of time, dear friends. Be on guard so that you will not be carried away by the errors of these wicked people and lose your own secure footing" (2 Peter 3:17 NLT). Following Christ means that we strap ourselves in and paddle against popular trends and ideals.

If we don't, we'll find ourselves spiritually lost at sea. The farther away from the Lord we get, the softer His voice becomes. Cultural trends, no matter how counterbiblical they may be, seep into the boat. The apostle Paul encourages us to stay tethered to Jesus:

> Then we will no longer be immature like children. We won't be tossed and blown about by every wind of new teaching. We will not be influenced when people try to trick us with lies so clever they sound like the truth (Eph. 4:14 NLT).

Why are we so prone to drifting? Because we are sinful by nature.

> The sinful nature wants to do evil, which is just the opposite of what the Spirit wants. And the Spirit gives us desires that are the opposite of what the sinful nature desires. These two forces are constantly fighting each other, so you are not free to carry out your good intentions.
>
> —Galatians 5:17 NLT

You and I will, inevitably, go through periods of drifting. Fortunately, Christ, our heavenly Coast Guard, is always waiting for our SOS call. Like the father with the prodigal son, He never stops scanning the horizon, hoping for His children to come home. He leaves the lighthouse on all night. Be encouraged; His forgiveness is a short prayer away. You cannot sail so far off course that His mercy can't reach you. Wear this truth like a life vest: there is far more grace in God than sin in you.

SALTY

You are the salt of the earth. But what good is salt if it
has lost its flavor? Can you make it salty again? It will
be thrown out and trampled underfoot as worthless.

—Matthew 5:13 NLT

If I were to compare myself to an item of food, I would have to choose
tofu. Much like the processed block of coagulated soy milk and bean
curd, I have a tendency to absorb the flavor of those around me. In sixth
grade, Karen (name changed) was the class queen bee. She wasn't the
most beautiful among us, though she had cool clothes. She wasn't the
most talented and she didn't come from the richest family, but it didn't
matter. She was the most popular, so when she said, "Jump!" we jumped.

Once every week or two, Karen would issue a declaration of
contempt. She was mad at so-and-so, and, therefore, any sheep in her
flock caught talking to the object of her anger would be banished to the
"nerdy table" at lunch. That was how it was, and no one rebelled against
her dictatorship style of governing.

It wasn't long before my name came up on the wheel of misfortune,
and there I sat, sack lunch before me, at the dreaded table. I had never
experienced anything like it. None of my friends would look at me.
There was no one to sit with on the bus, and no one to skip rope with at
recess. I was completely alone.

Eventually, my transgressions were forgiven, and I was welcomed
back into the fold as another sadly took my place in exile. I remember
how hurtful it was. I keenly recall not liking Karen and not wanting to
be a part of her "group" anymore. I wish I could tell you I stuck up for

the misfortunate one of the moment, but I didn't. I followed our fickle shepherd right along with the rest of the bleating lambs.

In sixth grade, it was Karen. The summer between my freshman and sophomore years of high school, it was a football player. I had a mad crush, and he had bad intentions. Not wanting to seem lame, I let him convince me to drink. He and his buddy cheered me on as I tilted back a bottle of whisky and downed it like a dying man in the desert—an escapade that bought me an ambulance ride and cost me my dignity.

Later in life, alcohol became the theme of everything I did. Even when I didn't want to drink, it took no arm twisting to coax me. One margarita led to two, then three, and three led to trouble. When God made it clear that my partying days were over, He allowed me to see the moldable mess I'd become. He put me through a painful pruning process, cutting away unhealthy relationships and grafting in new ones.

I still have moldable mess moments, and I still sometimes look like tofu. I regularly check my absorption rate. Am I becoming too peppery? Too bitter? Am I sickeningly sweet and insincere? All of us are impressionable and, left unchecked, adopt the traits of those around us. That's why it's crucial that we know the Bible. We must faithfully attend Bible-teaching churches. Jesus wants us to place our messy selves in His hands and trust Him with the molding process.

What is shaping you? What kind of flavor do you bring? Jesus says Christians should be salty.

Every now and then, I'll commit an afternoon to making chicken and dumplings from scratch. Just before adding the dumplings, I always taste the soup.

Not bad, just a little bland, I thought to myself awhile back. The recipe makes a five-quart dish, so I added a half-teaspoon of salt, stirred it up, and tasted it again. *Perfect!* It is amazing how a small amount of salt can make such a difference to so much soup.

God is calling each one of us to be influential, purposeful Christians. He has blessed me with some wonderfully salty friendships to help along the way—Melissa, who is patient and kind; Sandi, a mighty prayer-warrior for her friends; Anne, rich in wisdom and loyal as the day is long; and Michelle, an accomplished speaker/author with a heart for the hurting. Because of their faith and obedience, I have a better marriage and a better relationship with Jesus. I make better choices for my children, and I have resolved to influence rather than be influenced.

> You are the light of the world—like a city on a hilltop
> that cannot be hidden.

> —Matthew 5:14 NLT

Jesus calls each one of us to make a choice. Are you the dough or the yeast? The soup or the salt? An intentional Christian, seeking to lead others to Christ, or a benchwarmer, watching others fight from the sidelines?

Be salty. Love on purpose. Serve with joy. Shine brightly. Don't let a day go by without doing *something* to bring glory to the Kingdom of God. Get off of the bleachers and into the game. Invite a friend to church. Join a Bible study. Speak words of comfort and encouragement. And above all else, shine for the One that makes the soup.

> Arise, Jerusalem! Let your light shine for all to see. For
> the glory of the Lord rises to shine on you. Darkness as
> black as night covers all the nations of the earth, but the
> glory of the Lord rises and appears over you. All nations
> will come to your light; mighty kings will come to see
> your radiance.

> —Isaiah 60: 1–3 NLT

UMBRELLA HOLDER

Moses' arms soon became so tired he could no longer hold them up. So Aaron and Hur found a stone for him to sit on. Then they stood on each side of Moses, holding up his hands. So his hands held steady until sunset. As a result, Joshua overwhelmed the army of Amalek in battle.

—Exodus 17:12–13 NLT

We are not meant to bear burdens alone.

This was never more clearly illustrated to me than in November of 2010. I was serving on a ministry called Thirsty Thursday/First Friday Feast. A rotating panel of speakers would present a Christ-centered talk with a light meal on the first Thursday and Friday of every month. In November, one of our speakers—we'll call her Jane—shared a very moving testimony.

She had chosen to leave a lucrative, high-profile job in corporate America to be home with her family. Then the economy crumbled. Her husband owns and operates a company that works directly with home builders, so when home sales dropped, so did his business. They went through their savings, then their 401K. As their income shrank and their bills grew, they realized they would have to sell their house.

And then it rained, and rained, and rained.

That's when their problems *really* began. Somewhere in their roof was a hole. It's an easy fix if you can find it, but they couldn't find it. The roof only leaked when it rained in a certain direction, and no one could pinpoint it. Not many people are interested in a house with a leak and extensive water damage, so they couldn't sell. But they also couldn't afford the payments, so they sank further and further into debt.

Then their son was mugged. Then her husband's equipment was stolen. My sweet friend tried desperately to find a full-time job with benefits in the midst of the worst economic slide since the Great Depression with no luck.

She shouldered this alone until November of 2010. When she gave her heartfelt, tear-filled story, every woman in the audience sat motionless, hanging on her every word. Her display of faith through the storm inspired one woman after another to come forward with their stories, and Jane discovered that she wasn't quite as alone as she thought. Afterward, she received a flood of e-mails offering prayers and suggestions. Someone came and looked at her roof for free. In an effort to help with her job search, friends sent connections and networking opportunities, and slowly, the tide began to turn.

She is not the only one who has fought to stay afloat in a storm.

My struggle with alcohol spanned twenty-two years, from my first taste of champagne at thirteen to my last martini at thirty-five. One day, a girlfriend and I were out walking. No longer able to keep silent, I nervously confided in her about my drinking.

"I think I'm supposed to stop," I said, "but I'm scared to death." She listened quietly, gave me a hug, and told me she loved me.

A few days later, she called to tell me that God had laid it on her heart that I should stop drinking immediately.

"I will help you in any way I can," she said, "but you have to step out in faith that He will see you through this." I didn't stop that day, but she was the catalyst that began my recovery. The first few months of living alcohol-free were both difficult and frightening, but my husband, sisters, parents, and friends rallied around me, holding up my arms when waves of temptation hit.

God does not mean for us to bear our burdens alone.

I believe with all my heart that God strengthens us to weather storms and shelters us in the midst of them. But I also believe He charges us to hold each other's umbrellas.

Two people are better off than one, for they can help each other succeed. If one person falls, the other can reach out and help. But someone who falls alone is in real trouble.

—Ecclesiastes 4:9–10 NLT

We were not meant to exist in isolation. We were created to love God and one another as well as to serve God and one another. I treasure every opportunity to hold someone's umbrella. Just as Aaron and Hur strengthened Moses by holding up his arms, we strengthen each other by listening, by simple acts of service, and with our presence. We are closest to Christ when we allow Him to work through us. Jesus sends His Spirit, but as believers, we are His body. We are the arms that hug and the hands that heal. We are His mouthpiece, sharing the good news of the gospel, but the news is meant to be lived out. This is the heart and soul of Christianity: that we would introduce people to Christ with our love and sacrificial service. We may or may not win them over with our words, but who can resist His love?

Who in your life needs an umbrella holder?

Share each other's burdens, and in this way obey the law of Christ.

—Galatians 6:2 NLT

APPLE PIE

O taste and see that the Lord is good.

—Psalm 34:8a NASB

Growing up, my family lived somewhat of a nomadic lifestyle, moving approximately every three years. I was born in Illinois. We celebrated my second birthday in New Town Square, Pennsylvania, and my fifth in New Brighton, Minnesota. I started fourth grade in Overland Park, Kansas, and finished seventh grade in Shoreview, Minnesota. Never ones to stay put, we moved to Highlands Ranch, Colorado, in the middle of my sophomore year of high school. After I graduated, I packed up and headed to the University of Kansas while the rest of my family loaded the minivan, said good-bye to yet another home, and drove northeast. They parked their car in Shoreview for the second time, and that is where my sisters graduated from high school.

Nomads.

We lived near family once when we were in Colorado. Everyone else was spread out. Several times a year, my maternal grandmother would come for a nice, long stay. While she was with us, she was typically hard at work at one of two things: sewing or baking.

Grandma Williams makes heavenly apple pies— buttery, flakey crust and crisp, juicy apples baked to just the right consistency with the perfect blend of sugar and cinnamon. Her pies are more than dessert; they're an experience. Life was fine before her apple pie, but once I tried it, life was better.

In high school, no longer satisfied with pie once or twice a year, I commissioned grandma to teach me the secret recipe. Now I can have that pie whenever I want (and have three to four hours to spend making it—grandma's pie is a labor of love).

O taste and see that the Lord is good.

—Psalm 34:8a NASB

When we discover something wonderful, our first thought is to tell someone—to invite someone to experience it with us. My husband does it all the time at restaurants: "Bec! You have to try this lasagna. It's the best!" Or, "Oh, taste this chocolate cake. You'll die." I love how David, the psalms' author, has the same excited urgency as he invites us to know our God.

In Hebrew, the word for *taste* is *taam (taw-am')*. It also means "to perceive with your senses."[1]

The Hebrew word for *see* is elsewhere used for "approve, encountered, enjoy, experience, indeed look and keep on looking."[2] David's language implies great excitement; he is issuing an invitation to "try it," certain that once you experience it, you will not want to go back to the state you were in before you knew it. It denotes a continuing action, meaning, "keep on experiencing it!" It is also translated as "tell." I believe that David is issuing an invitation, with great enthusiasm, to know God on a deeper level, knowing that once we do, our souls will keep coming back for more. Here is a little secret I learned from David: the more you experience God, the more God you need, and the more God you get, the more you want others to experience Him too.

How blessed is the man who takes refuge in Him!

—Psalm 34:8b NASB

---

[1] NAS Exhaustive Concordance of the Bible with Hebrew-Aramaic and Greek Dictionaries
Copyright © 1981, 1998 by The Lockman Foundation
All rights reserved Lockman.org

[2] See 1

Oh, that we would get more excited about God and what He is doing than an apple pie. I confess that I have probably issued more invitations to taste a dessert than I have my Lord and Savior. I've been more excited about new shoes than bringing a friend to church. How sad that we would place such importance on ordinary things. Shoes offer fleeting happiness. Jesus promises eternal salvation.

I would like to make a gentle suggestion. If you are bored with your faith, perhaps it's been too long since you experienced Jesus. King David urges us to move beyond dutiful prayer and weekly church attendance. David beckons us to encounter Him. To encounter Him, we must actively seek Him through faithful study of His Word.

> "If you look for me wholeheartedly, you will find me. I will be found by you," says the Lord. "I will end your captivity and restore your fortunes. I will gather you out of the nations where I sent you and will bring you home again to your own land."

> —Jeremiah 29:13–14 NLT

This is a promise of adventure! Taste His goodness and see for yourself. He will end your boredom and restore your hope. He will gather you to Himself, revealing more and more of His Spirit as you ask Him to.

> How sweet are Your words to my taste! Yes, sweeter than honey to my mouth!

> —Psalm 119:103 NASB

BROKEN BONES

God's love was revealed among us in this way: God
sent His One and Only Son into the world so that we
might live through Him. Love consists in this: not that
we loved God, but that He loved us and sent His Son to
be the propitiation for our sins.

—1 John 4:9–10 HCSB

I've suffered a few broken bones in my day. Most from distance running:
two stress fractures along my lower fibula (ankle) and one shattered
medial sesamoid in the bottom of my right foot. I also experienced
the pleasure of a cracked metatarsal (top of the foot), courtesy of
an overserved and overzealous cowboy who stepped on me while
attempting to dance.

In October of 2011, my sweet daughter fell off the monkey bars on
the playground and broke her wrist. Visibly. *Very* visibly.

I rushed to the school nurse's office, then to our pediatrician. One
look (more of a grimace) at Caitlyn's arm, and the doctor set down her
chart.

"Christine," she called, "please set an appointment for Caitlyn with
one of our orthopedic surgeons." My throat swelled as my stomach sank.
She confirmed what I had already guessed. "I don't need to x-ray this
to know it's broken. She will likely need this reset as soon as possible,
so we're going to find an ortho to see her today."

I nodded.

"Nothing else to eat or drink," she continued.

More nodding.

"Any questions?"

Still not trusting myself to speak, I shook my head. She smiled and kissed Caitlyn's cheek. "You'll be just fine, sweetheart," she said softly.

I hugged my daughter close. "Honey, we're going to see another doctor now, and they're going to fix those bones right up." Looking very pale, Caitlyn smiled feebly.

A few hours later, we pulled into the orthopedics office and, after a brief wait, sat down with the doctor. He opened his laptop and showed us the x-ray.

"You can see here there is a twenty-seven degree break on this bone," he stated, using his pen as a pointer. "It can't stay that way." Seemingly unable to do anything else, I nodded. "I've contacted the surgical center, and if you get her there at 5:45 a.m., I'll snap it back into place before I start the day's surgeries."

A few more instructions were given, and we headed home. Caitlyn was all smiles now with a new stuffed monkey and a Ring Pop. The anesthesiologist (who, by God's favor, was a friend from church) called that evening to go over preoperative instructions one more time. I carefully laid out a comfy outfit for my daughter and tucked her into bed.

The next morning, we pulled into the surgery center at 5:43 a.m.

As I stated before, I'm no stranger to broken bones and how they hurt.

I would gladly take a sledgehammer to every bone in my body to save my sweet girl the pain she went through that morning.

As the nurse brought me back to the recovery area, I could hear my baby shrieking. I raced in the room to find another nurse holding her down as she fought and kicked hysterically.

"I'm here, sweetheart. Mommy's here!" Caitlyn was screaming, retching, and clenching her teeth. She couldn't put a sentence together, only mustering, "Hurts! Hurts! Mommy! Hurts!"

I asked the nurse about pain medication and was answered with a woeful look and a shaking head. After ten more minutes (that felt like eternity) the surgeon walked over. He agreed to another dose of Tylenol/Codeine, and after fifteen more minutes, the nurse returned with the medicine.

God, I prayed silently, *give me the pain! Take it away from my daughter, and give the pain to me!* The sight of my shaking, sobbing baby girl on that cold, metal hospital gurney was almost too much to bear. At that moment, I would've done absolutely anything to end her suffering.

> When Jesus therefore saw her weeping, and the Jews who came with her also weeping, He was deeply moved in spirit and was troubled, and said, "Where have you laid him?" They said to Him, "Lord, come and see." Jesus wept.
>
> —John 11:33–35 NASB

Every now and then, through everyday circumstances, I feel as though God gives me a glimpse into His heart. As I sat there, holding my wailing daughter, I thought of Jesus, entering time and space to walk with us, talk to us, heal us, and suffer for us. He did this not because He had to, but because He chose to, hoping we might choose Him in return. He wants you to know Him, and He wants you to know that *He knows.* He knows the depths of our sorrow. He feels our hurt. He knows that life is difficult, and He wants you to know that there is more.

> Now since the children have flesh and blood in common, Jesus also shared in these, so that through His death He might destroy the one holding the power of death—that is, the Devil—and free those who were held in slavery all their lives by the fear of death.
>
> —Hebrews 2:14–15 HCSB

I picture God in the heavens, watching us as I watched my daughter. And while I was unable to ease her pain, Jesus Christ stepped off the throne and heaped suffering on Himself so that we might be saved.

In his marvelous book *And the Angels Were Silent,* author and pastor Max Lucado writes, "He would rather go to hell for you than go to heaven without you."

Think about that for a moment. Don't skip to the next sentence. Don't let your thoughts wander to other things.

"He would rather go to hell *for* you than go to heaven *without* you."

Please don't take that for granted. Jesus loved you enough to bear every whiplash, every thorn, every blow, and every nail.

Caitlyn's bone went back into place nicely, and after a morning spent vomiting from the anesthesia, she curled up on the couch with her monkey, her blankie, and a movie. The worst was over, and now she scarcely remembers the incident.

One day, when we sit at the heavenly banquet with eternity stretched out before us, we will recall this life as one remembers a broken bone from their childhood. Did it hurt? Yes. But in the grand scheme of things, it was little more than a blip on the radar.

Jesus' work on the cross ensures our seat at the table. His blood covers our sinfulness. He gives us His robes of righteousness. His perfect sacrifice was sufficient, and heaven waits for those who have received Him.

MADDIE

We reject all shameful deeds and underhanded methods. We don't try to trick anyone or distort the word of God. We tell the truth before God, and all who are honest know this.

—2 Corinthians 4:2 NLT

If it weren't for a girl named Maddie, I might throw in the towel and give up. Well, not really, but I would think about it.

Maddie is an eighteen-year-old girl in my Sunday school class. A class, by the way, consisting mainly of thirty- to sixty-something-year-old married couples. That doesn't bother her a bit. She shows up faithfully every week, Bible open and questions ready.

Maddie has a heart for Jesus. She also has a heart to reach her generation for Christ. I pray that God will use this tiny, long-haired, blue-eyed young woman in a mighty way because Maddie's generation, and our country in general, is in a lot of trouble.

In 2012, researchers from the University of California, Berkeley, and Duke University released a study showing that religious affiliation in America is at an all-time low. Approximately one out every five US citizens claims no church or religious affiliation. In other words, 20% of Americans no longer see religion as valuable. More troubling to me is Lifeway Research's report on the millennial generation (those born between 1980 and 2000). In their study titled *The Millennials*, authors Thom Rainey and Jess Rainer conclude that a mere 13% of millennials consider religion, of any type, important.

If this is true, we are doing something wrong. Terribly wrong.

I have loved you even as the Father has loved me.
Remain in my love.

—John 15:9 NLT

Maddie takes her relationship with Jesus seriously. She reads the Scriptures and lives them out. Many times over the past few years, she has shown up early with her Bible, a tattered copy of Lee Strobel's *Case for Christ,* and a list of names to pray for.

Maddie understands the nature of her peers. They are thinkers who value education, social justice, and truth. Many of them think God, Santa, and the Tooth Fairy have one thing in common: they're cute when you're a kid, but they are no more real than magic beans.

Maddie isn't afraid of their questions. She welcomes open discussion and doesn't duck when they doubt. Instead, she prepares herself and has an answer ready to go.

Instead, you must worship Christ as Lord of your
life. And if someone asks about your Christian hope,
always be ready to explain it. But do this in a gentle and
respectful way.

—2 Peter 3:15–16a NLT

What would you say if someone asked you why you believe in Jesus?
I was listening to a Q & A session with a well-known pastor from a well-known church. He answered theological and doctrinal questions in a clear, concise way, and his love for Christ was obvious. He quoted Scripture as though he'd memorized the Bible. He was energetic and engaging. And then, the question.

A young man explained how he had gone to church his entire life. He knew the Ten Commandments and the Lord's Prayer. He'd been sprinkled as an infant and dunked at twelve. But he didn't believe that Jesus was God, and he wasn't buying what Christians were selling.

"How do you know it's real?" the young man asked. "Why are you so sure that Jesus is the only way to heaven?"

The good pastor promptly rattled off several verses about faith and salvation.

And then, the next question came.

"But I don't believe that the Bible is true," the young man bravely insisted. "Is there anything else that proves Jesus is God?"

Silence.

"Well," the pastor finally stammered, "you know, you just have to have faith and believe. You have to read the Bible and have faith that it's true."

I sat there, dumbfounded. This young man had excellent questions and a heart longing for certainty, and all he got was "read the Bible and believe?"

That might have worked for you and me, but it's a new day, and this generation is not satisfied with "you gotta have faith."

They want proof.

And Maddie would tell them there is no shortage of proof.

> Therefore the Lord Himself will give you a sign: Behold, a virgin will be with child and bear a son, and she will call His name Immanuel.
>
> —Isaiah 7:14 NASB

> Now all this took place to fulfill what was spoken by the Lord through the prophet: "See, the virgin will become pregnant and give birth to a son, and they will name Him Immanuel," which is translated "God is with us."
>
> —Matthew 1:22–23 HCSB

Every mainstream religion has sacred writings. The Bible is the only collection that has the audacity to claim it predicts the future. The crazier part is that it does.

The book of Isaiah has more Messianic prophecies than any other book in the Old Testament. The prophet ministered through the reigns of Judean kings Uzzia, Jotham, Ahaz, and Hezekiah. His ministry spanned over forty decades, between 740–697 BC, and scholars estimate that the book was penned no later than 680 BC.

An encyclopedia (if you can find one) will confirm an entire scroll of Isaiah was uncovered with the Dead Sea Scrolls in 1948, along with over eight hundred manuscripts of every book in the Old Testament, save Esther. The scrolls are dated around 200 BC.

Why is that important?

It's important because science and archeology together prove that the book of Isaiah (and the Old Testament) was written over two hundred years before Jesus' feet touched earthen soil.

That's what I want my kids to know. That's what Maddie understands. It's not enough for us to teach our children to believe in Jesus. We need to explain why they should believe in Jesus.

They need cold, hard facts.

Here's one: it is almost mathematically impossible for Jesus to be anyone other than who He says He is. Dr. David R. Reagan of *Lamb and Lion Ministries* quotes the work of Prof. Peter Stoner in his book, *Science Speaks.* According to Dr. Reagan, Prof. Stoner used a mathematical analysis to determine the odds that Christ would fulfill eight prophecies at once. His conclusion was almost one out of one-hundred-quadrillion. Since you've likely never seen that number, it looks like this: 100,000,000,000,000,000.[3]

That is the likelihood that Jesus would fulfill eight prophecies at the same time by random chance.

He fulfilled over three hundred perfectly and indisputably. I would write out the probability, except I don't have enough room, so let's just agree that mathematics testify to the divinity of Christ.

This generation needs to understand that the Bible is the authoritative, authentic, inerrant Word of God. The Bible we have today has been meticulously preserved through the centuries by scribes spending painstakingly long hours copying each page one letter at a time. Rick Warren addresses this in his Bible study, *40 Days in the Word*. The scribes never wrote from memory. They knew precisely how many

---

[3]   Reagan, Dr. David R. "Applying the Science of Probability to the Scriptures." *LambLion.com.*
http://www.lamblion.com/articles/articles_bible6.php. 03 August 2014

columns each scroll must have, the exact length of each column (no less than forty-eight lines, no more than sixty), and the breadth of each column (exactly thirty letters).[4] The Scriptures contain a less than 5% margin of error, and the "errors" are mainly switched letters, which never affect doctrinal issues, like salvation.

And then there's the cost. Just as our salvation was purchased with blood, so was the Bible.

Eleven of the twelve apostles died horrific, torturous deaths, preferring martyrdom to denying Jesus. Through the centuries, countless others have done the same to carry the gospel to the ends of the earth.

Why would they do that if they didn't know with absolute certainty that Jesus is God? Why would they subject themselves to every kind of humiliation, despicable acts beyond description, if every "god" got them to heaven?

If every religion is right, why would God send His Son to die on a cross?

In the 1520s a man named William Tyndale worked in secret to translate the entire New Testament from Greek to English. He completed the project in February 1526, only to learn that Bishop Cuthbert Tunstall planned to buy all six-thousand copies and burn them at his church.

Tyndale found out about Tunstall's scheme and went along with it. He charged the Bishop a great amount of money, paid his debts, and started over with his earnings, confident that the second version would be better than the first.

For his efforts and accomplishments, Tyndale was rewarded with a life on the lam; betrayal was followed by arrest, and he was ultimately tied to a stake, strangled by his executioner, and burned.[5]

We can buy a Bible for five dollars, while martyrs like Tyndale paid for it with their lives.

Why would Tyndale and countless others have gone to those lengths if the gospel was a fairy tale? What in the world would convince them

---

4   Warren, Rick M. "40 Days in the Word: Workbook." Rancho Santa Margarita: Saddleback Resources, 2011. Print.

5   http://www.christianitytoday.com/ch/131christians/scholarsandscientists/tyndale.html; http://www.tyndalearchive.com/Brewer/Alice/WilliamT.htm

to sacrifice a comfortable life for laborious work that brought no earthly reward?

Jesus.

One glimpse at God in His glory, and Isaiah cried out, saying, "It's all over! I am doomed, for I am a sinful man. I have filthy lips, and I live among a people with filthy lips. Yet I have seen the King, the Lord of Heaven's Armies" (Isa. 6:5 NLT).

When Peter realized who Jesus was, he fell to his knees and said, "Oh, Lord, please leave me—I'm too much of a sinner to be around you" (Luke 5:8 NLT).

Confronted with the risen Christ on the road to Damascus, Paul fell flat on his face and went from devastating the Christian movement to leading it (Acts 9).

And when John, the "one Jesus loved," the one who sat at His feet and rested on His chest, saw his Lord in His resurrected state, he "fell at His feet" as though dead (Rev. 1:17).

Each of us will, at some point, confront this same risen Christ, and each of us will be called to give an account of our lives. No matter what kind of life we lived, if we aren't covered by His grace, we're naked in our shame.

Jesus is real. The cross happened. He loves you. And be assured, He is coming back. So let's link arms with Maddie and do something about it.

> In those days John the Baptist came to the Judean wilderness and began preaching. His message was, "Repent of your sins and turn to God, for the Kingdom of Heaven is near." The prophet Isaiah was speaking about John when he said, "He is a voice shouting in the wilderness, 'Prepare the way for the Lord's coming! Clear the road for him!'"
>
> —Matthew 3:1–3 NLT

HOOKY

And let us consider how we may spur one another on toward love and good deeds, not giving up meeting together, as some are in the habit of doing, but encouraging one another—and all the more as you see the Day approaching.

—Hebrews 10:24–25 NIV

I skipped church one Sunday.

Big deal, you might be thinking. *People skip church all the time.*

Not me. I love our church. I love my Sunday school class. I love the friendships my husband and I have made that are built on and center around Christ. I love the staff, and I love the teachers who faithfully teach my children the Word of God each week.

I rarely skip, but this time, I did.

There was no particular reason; I just didn't feel like going. I had all the excuses I needed: a poor night's sleep, exhausted after a week of serving in several other ministries, and I just wanted a morning where I didn't have to rush.

My husband was going to skip with me until our daughter came bounding down the stairs with her clothes and shoes on, hair and teeth brushed, and her eyes and smile sparkling. Mike looked at me and shook his head.

"I can't disappoint her," he said. "You stay home. You've earned a day off."

Done.

As Mike and Caitlyn left, Nick and I packed up the stroller. To ease my nagging conscience, I loaded a sermon on my iPod and away we went. Jog to the park, play awhile, then jog home.

With every plodding step, the guilt increased. I glanced at the time: 9:37a.m. At that moment, I knew the praise team was leading worship. I pictured the congregation with lifted hands, voices filling the sanctuary with songs of adoration, and I felt the searing stab of conviction slicing through my conscience. I thought about the work our pastor put into the sermon, pouring his heart and soul into the words, praying for the church as he sought the Holy Spirit. I remembered my neighbor and the conversation we'd had the other day. I had spent ten minutes telling her about my church and convincing her to give it a try. I imagined her sitting there with her children, not knowing anyone and wondering where I was.

That was the knockout punch to the soul.

By the time my husband and daughter arrived home, I was miserable. Mike didn't help.

"Everyone wanted to know where you were!" he said happily as he walked through the door.

All day long, I felt awful.

Why does it matter to God whether or not we go to church? I can praise Him by myself in the car. I can read the Bible on my own, and I can listen to sermons all day long. Why does God care so much about gathering in a public place to worship?

Because we are the body of Christ.

> Just as our bodies have many parts and each part has
> a special function, so it is with Christ's body. We are
> many parts of one body, and we all belong to each other.
>
> —Romans 12:4–5 NLT

We need each other. We need each other's prayers and encouragement. We need to laugh together, and sometimes need to weep together. God did not design us to face life on our own; we need friendship and fellowship. More than anything else, in this day and in these times, we need to meet with others who are striving to make one name great: Jesus Christ.

My pastor phrases it this way: "We need to be with the body of Christ because His Spirit is multiplied when we gather."

Jesus told His disciples that "where two or three gather together as my followers, I am there among them" and God's economy is not like ours (Mt. 18:20 NLT). When we give God our money, He increases it to accomplish His purposes. When we offer our time, He does the same. And when we come together as His body, He fills us far beyond what the containers of our hearts can hold.

We were made to worship. The more we praise Him, the more we experience Him. The more we experience Him, the more of Him we want, and the more Jesus we want, the more Jesus we get. The more Jesus we get, the more Jesus we share, and we find ourselves living smack in the center of His will. What a lovely place to be!

> How lovely is your dwelling place, O Lord of Heaven's Armies. I long, yes, I faint with longing to enter the courts of the Lord. With my whole being, body and soul, I will shout joyfully to the living God.
>
> —Psalm 84: 1–2 NLT

It occurred to me while playing hooky how humankind tends to busy itself. We make appointments for the doctor, the dentist, our hair, and nails. We set dates with our spouses, our friends, and our clients or coworkers. But when it comes to meeting with Jesus, either in the Bible, quiet time, or public worship, we fit Him in when we feel like it. We make excuses, chasing fleeting happiness instead of the only One that satisfies our souls.

Let us not neglect our meeting together.

> Better a day in Your courts than a thousand anywhere else. I would rather be at the door of the house of my God than to live in the tents of wicked people. For the Lord God is a sun and shield. The Lord gives grace

and glory; He does not withhold the good from those who live with integrity. Happy is the person who trusts in You, Lord of Hosts!

—Psalm 84: 10–12 HCSB

THE RED LIGHT

It is He who sits above the circle of the earth, and its inhabitants are like grasshoppers, who stretches out the heavens like a curtain and spreads them out like a tent to dwell in.

—Isaiah 40:22 NASB

Do you like the window or the aisle seat?

I am a window girl myself, and anytime I have a choice when flying, that's what I pick. Many people like the aisle, appreciating the easy access in and out of their row, but I'll trade the convenience for the view any day.

My favorite moment of the journey is when the plane and ground part. One moment, you are hurtling forward at breakneck speed and the next, buildings turn to boxes, and cars become ants as the earth shrinks to dollhouse-sized proportions below. The horizon goes on for miles and miles when you're gazing at it from the window seat of a plane in flight.

Something else happens when I'm looking down from thirty-thousand feet. Somehow, as we soar through the clouds, as I marvel at the curvature of the earth and the God who created it, my worries and concerns seem smaller too.

It's all a matter of perspective.

This was illustrated perfectly on the way home from the gym one day.

Our gym is less than three miles from our house. The drive takes anywhere from five to fifteen minutes, depending on traffic. The route includes two major intersections. You know the type: five lanes across, including two left turn lanes, two center lanes, and a lane for turning right.

I sat there in the right left-turn lane late one afternoon in 108 degree heat with two grouchy kids and a reluctant air conditioner. I looked out of my window and watched a young woman texting on her phone. To my right was a minivan. I nodded in understanding to the frazzled mother in the driver's seat, and she half-smiled back.

I glanced at the clock on my dash, certain at least ten minutes had passed, but no. Just three.

As the cars in the two center lanes inched forward, I craned my neck, straining to see the flash of green signaling my freedom, but the left lanes were still red. I sighed and leaned back in resignation. Breaking through my haze like an angry drill sergeant, my son hollered, "Mo-om! Go!"

I took a deep breath and shook my head, too hot and tired to respond.

"Mo-om," he cried again. "Why don't you go?!"

"Nick," I calmly replied, "I can't go. We're at a red light." Right then, the arrow switched from red to green, but the line was long, and my turn wouldn't come for another cycle. Nick, not privy to the cars in front of us yelled, "Now you can go—*go!*"

I sat there, silently willing the traffic to move. Glancing in the rearview mirror, I stifled my laughter at the serious look on my son's face. With his little brow furrowed and jaw clenched, he looked like a miniature version of a frustrated professor trying to get his class to understand, but it was Nick who could not understand. You see, from the back seat, he had a limited perspective. I was in the front seat with the panoramic view. His view was hindered; he couldn't see the whole picture. He only knew that other cars were moving while we sat still.

> For the Lord gives wisdom; from His mouth come knowledge and understanding.
>
> —Proverbs 2:6 NASB

What if I had agreed to go when my son asked me to? I would have driven straight into the rear bumper of the car in front of me. Being three at the time, Nick didn't have the insight or understanding to navigate us safely home. He needed a driver with a front-seat perspective.

God can supernaturally impart wisdom to us any time He desires. In my experience, though, wisdom comes as He changes our perspective through time and experience.

This also proved true in my career. I got my first job in radio in late 1998, and the only thing in the world I wanted was a spot on a morning show. In my naivety (or arrogance) I thought I was ready. Now when I look back, I see it differently. Had God answered my prayers and opened the door to a prime time position, I would have failed. I didn't understand timing or pacing. I was a terrible "self-editor." If you want a job in a major market (like Dallas), you need to grasp the concepts of "running a tight board" and finding "the right exit ramp." I had much to learn about things not taught in the classroom.

To put it simply, I needed experience. I needed the grueling spring and summer of 1999, where I learned the basics while working the overnight shift. I needed the following two-and-a-half years spent working nights with an experienced cohost. Melinda Dickerson taught me a treasure trove of radio tips during that period. When a morning-show position opened up, I was ready.

> Those who trust their own insight are foolish, but anyone who walks in wisdom is safe.
>
> —Proverbs 28:26 NLT

We don't have a bird's eye view of life. We see one direction at a time, and our vision is clouded with bias. Our wisdom is limited to our experience, but even our memories are unreliable. We desperately need a shepherd.

God, in His great love and mercy, did not plunk us down on our planet and leave us to our own devices. He gave His law to Moses and reiterated it to the prophets. He sent His Son that we might know that we are not alone, and He gave us His Word: the Bible. His Holy Spirit is our constant companion, gently nudging and guiding us in the right direction. When times are difficult—and there will be difficult times—we must remember that His perspective is better than ours. He sees around the corner and knows what is next. When we suffer, we can be comforted knowing that nothing gets to us without first passing through His hands. His timing is impeccable; He knows just the right moment to pull us from the fire. His plan is perfect, and every trial He allows is refining us.

At times, the path will be rocky and the road will be steep. Cling to Him, for as long as you do, you might stumble, but you will never, ever fall.

> For He will conceal me in His shelter in the day of adversity; He will hide me under the cover of His tent; He will set me high on a rock.

> —Proverbs 27:5 HCSB

THE CURVE

If the law could give us new life, we could be made right
with God by obeying it. But the Scriptures declare that
we are all prisoners of sin, so we receive God's promise
of freedom only by believing in Jesus Christ.

—Galatians 3:21b–22 NLT

Have you ever rooted for someone to fail? I have.

Oh, I don't like admitting that.

As a freshman at Mounds View High School, I hoped against hope
that a girl named Tish would have a lousy audition so that I would win
the role of Adelaide in *Guys & Dolls*. She had a fantastic tryout and got
the part. The night before the show, I secretly wanted her to get sick, so
I, being her understudy, could fill in. She showed up, knocked it out of
the park, and received a standing ovation, while I forced a smile from
the chorus line.

As a sophomore at our school's talent show, I listened with white-
knuckled intensity as Sara sang a Whitney Houston ballad, waiting for
a massive mistake that never came. Her rendition of "Didn't We Almost
Have It All" far outshone my attempt at "Let's Hear it for the Boy," and
the trophy was hers.

It wasn't that I had a personal vendetta against them. It's just that
when they looked bad, I looked better.

It's kind of like grading on the curve.

Grading on the curve means that the worse the brainiacs do, the
better the slackers look. If the highest score on a test is 91, then 91
becomes 100%. Getting a teacher who subscribed to curve-driven

95

grading was like finding gold to someone like me: someone who did pretty well at all things creative but wrestled with math and science. When test time rolled around, there I was again, rooting for others to fail so that I would pass.

Surely we don't do that now. Or do we? Is it possible that, without meaning to, we grade ourselves on our own self-made curve, one that makes us look better when others look bad?

I bet I'm not the only blogger to feel a ping of envy when someone else's post goes viral. I push it away as quickly as I can, but that doesn't stop it from bubbling up in the first place. Have you ever avoided someone because you don't want to hear another happy story about their wonderful, perfect life? Have you ever stood next to another woman and suddenly felt frumpy? Or fat? Or like your accomplishments paled in comparison to hers?

What man hasn't secretly sized up another man's car? Or house? Or job? Or felt letdown when "Joe Success" gets another bonus twice as big as the last?

Curve-driven self-esteem isn't new—the Pharisees had it too.

> Then Jesus told this story to some who had great confidence in their own righteousness and scorned everyone else: "Two men went to the Temple to pray. One was a Pharisee, and the other was a despised tax collector. The Pharisee stood by himself and prayed this prayer: 'I thank you, God, that I am not a sinner like everyone else. For I don't cheat, I don't sin, and I don't commit adultery. I'm certainly not like that tax collector! I fast twice a week, and I give you a tenth of my income.'
>
> "But the tax collector stood at a distance and dared not even lift his eyes to heaven as he prayed. Instead, he beat his chest in sorrow, saying, 'O God, be merciful to me, for I am a sinner.'"
>
> —Luke 18:9–13 NLT

The Pharisee loudly trumpets his accomplishments, and compares himself to a sinful tax collector to highlight his righteousness. But Jesus fails the religious man and gives the tax collector an A.

Why?

Because Jesus doesn't look at the scorecard; He looks at the heart.

That one time you were secretly glad when that one person stumbled? He saw. The stifled jealousy? He knows. The not-so-pure motives? The thing you don't want anyone to find out? The gossip wrapped in a prayer request? All our faults? All our failures?

He knows.

He hears.

He sees.

And He credits you with righteousness.

You see, God doesn't grade on the curve. He grades on the cross.

That means you get an A, not because you gave the homeless man a twenty when others walked on by, not because you volunteer more than your neighbor, not because you're nice to the person everyone else avoids, and not because of your perfect church attendance.

If you could earn the A, it would be about you, but it's not about you. It's about Him.

It's about Jesus, the cross, and the empty tomb. Because of Jesus, you have an Advocate standing at the right hand of God, swatting down the enemy's accusations. Because of the cross, you're forgiven and because of the empty tomb, you are free—free from comparison, from envy, free to stop measuring yourself against others and jockeying for position, free to abandon the curve and embrace the cross.

So let's stop looking around and start looking up.

The more we gaze upon the face of Christ, the more lovely He becomes. The more lovely He becomes, the more we let Him in. The more we let Him in, the more we share His heart, and the more we share His heart, the more like Him we become.

When we do this, we feel joy, peace, and love. And we start to get it.

It really *isn't* about us. It's about a Father who loves us so much He would let His Son die for us. It's about a Son who would rather go to the cross for you than spend eternity without you. It's about a Spirit who will never leave you, fail you, or forsake you.

It's about grace. You can't earn it, you can't buy it, and you can't get into to heaven without it.

Jesus took the test for you. He lived the perfect, sinless life and because He did, you get the A. With the A comes grace, with grace comes salvation, and with salvation comes eternal life.

All you have to do is receive it.

> "For this is the will of My Father, that everyone who beholds the Son and believes in Him will have eternal life, and I Myself will raise him up on the last day."
>
> —John 6:40 NASB

"LEVEL ZERO"

Your eternal word, O LORD, stands firm in heaven. Your faithfulness extends to every generation, as enduring as the earth you created.

—Psalm 119:89–90 NLT

I pulled into the parking lot with three minutes left. Sighing with relief, I jumped out of the car and locked the door. With long, purposeful strides, I made my way to the front of the elementary school. After signing in, I strategically placed my visitor's sticker on my shirt so that I wouldn't catch my hair. Smiling at the other mom waiting in the lobby, I sat down.

Since small talk ceased to exist with the smart phone, I made no attempt to engage. The other mom was busy reading, and I didn't want to interrupt. Wait, let's be honest. I wanted to check my e-mail. I pulled out my phone, but before I could click it on, the shuffling on the other side of the glass doors alerted me to the kindergarteners making their way toward the cafeteria. A glance at the clock told me it was 10:20—right on time.

My son, six at the time, didn't know I was coming. Actually, neither did I. But my schedule was light and, as luck would have it, so was the traffic. I successfully made it across the DFW area in 50 minutes. Not bad for the tail end of rush hour.

I waved at Nick as the students walked single file through the hall. I laughed when he cocked his head in amazement, as if to say, "Mom? Is that you?"

The door buzzed open, and my little boy flung himself into my arms.

"Hi, sweetie," I said. "I'm so excited to have lunch with you!"

We sat down side by side, and I peppered him with questions as he unpacked his shiny Cars lunch box.

"Are you having a good day, honey?"

"Uh-huh."

"Are you learning fun things?"

"Shray-mow fribing."

"That's okay, Nick, you can wait until you're done chewing."

A pause, a swallow, a sip of Capri-Sun, and then, "Rainbow writing!"

Between bites, my son pointed out his new friends. After a short while, the lights went down.

"Okay, children," a sweet voice sang out. "Talk time is over, and now it's time to finish our lunch."

Since Nick was my second child in school, I was well versed in the lunchtime routine. The children are given twenty-five minutes. They are allowed to talk quietly for the first fifteen. The remainder is to be spent in silence. However, Ms. Hale soon realized that it was a lofty goal for a room full of five- and six-year-olds.

"Level zero. Level zero, everybody!" Clearly the kids were registering too high on the volume system. "Level zero, Allison. Henry, level zero."

As soon as she had one section quieted down, giggles would erupt from another. "Ms. Rosendahl's class, level zero! Level zero, everybody. I don't want you to sit out at recess." Talking during quiet time carried a heavy penalty.

As I watched the teacher monitor the noise level, I laughed at the way the children needed to hear the message over and over again. "Level zero, kids." It took a near-constant reminder to keep them on track.

That sure sounds familiar. Sometimes I do okay. Other times, I'm a spiritual kindergartner, needing God's message on repeat.

> How long must I struggle with anguish in my soul, with sorrow in my heart every day? How long will my enemy have the upper hand?
>
> —Psalm 13:2 NLT

How many times must I hear it before I will remember that God is *for* me? That He is not a passive-aggressive God who enjoys toying with my emotions, taking pleasure in my insecurities? And how much longer until I actually act like it's true? How often must I hear that He loves me, that He longs for me when I wander, and delights when I return? How much longer will He listen to my endless list of cares and complaints before His patience runs out?

As long as it takes.

> But you, O Lord, are a God of compassion and mercy, slow to get angry and filled with unfailing love and faithfulness.

> —Psalm 86:16 NLT

I will give myself the same advice that I gave a friend who wrestles with the same demons.

God *is* for you. He has always been for you. He created you on purpose, deliberately designing you with a divine purpose in mind, and He has not forgotten you.

Your fearfulness and your faithlessness does not rattle Him. He does not need your praise or your prayers to accomplish His will.

He knows you have a mind given to worry; His Word contains over 365 reminders not to. He knows, in your frailty, that you can't always feel His presence. That's okay. His faithfulness has nothing to do with your feelings.

He knows you don't always want to worship. He is not lacking—heaven is filled with legions of angels unceasingly praising His name—but He beckons you to join in the chorus, knowing that it brings joy to your soul and peace to your heart.

He knows you so well. He knows your deepest wounds, the ones you seldom allow to graze your consciousness. He knows the hurts you can't remember that shape the behaviors you can't explain. He sees past your pride, your selfish motives, and your insincerity. When He looks at you, He sees the completed work on the cross.

And He smiles.

And He says, "This one is mine."

Beloved, there is more grace in Him than sin in you, and He will remind you as often as you need Him to.

TRUE NORTH

How can a young man keep his way pure? By keeping
Your word.

—Psalm 119:9 HCSB

Our society has lost its true north.

If you are a hiker or sailor, you likely know the difference between true north and magnetic north. If you are not a hiker or sailor but have the inclination to hike or sail to the North Pole (who doesn't?), you need to understand both concepts. Why? Because magnetic north may get you close, but it won't get you to your destination. To reach the North Pole, you need true north.

Ask someone how to find north, and they will probably hand you a compass (or pull up the compass app on their phone). A compass represents the world's solution to finding your way. There is a problem, though, if you are looking for the North Pole. The compass won't get you there. According to Cristen Conger's article on *How to Find True North,*[6] a compass "will take you to a point in the arctic regions of Canada that continually shifts location based on the activity of the Earth's magnetic fields."

When you follow a compass, you are at the mercy of the ever-changing magnetic fields. It works like this: the magnetized needle of the compass is attracted to the liquid iron in the earth's core. The iron

---

[6] Conger, Cristen. "How to Find True North" 25 March 2008. HowStuffWorks. com. <http://adventure.howstuffworks.com/survival/wilderness/true-north. htm> 03 August 2014.

creates a horizontal magnetic field that pulls the needle to magnetic north.

True north is different. True north is the concept of moving from the South Pole to the North Pole in a straight line, illustrated in the lines of longitude. This is far more reliable because the North and South poles are constant. If you were to chart a course using both true and magnetic north, you would have two different routes. According to Conger, the discrepancy "is called the magnetic declination and is measured by the angle between true north and magnetic north when plotted on a map."

The variances are different depending on your location. For instance, in Arlington, Texas, magnetic north is 3° 55' east of true north; in Iceland it's -13° 9' west.

So what in the world does this have to do with us? A lot.

> I have chosen the faithful way; I have placed Your ordinances before me.
>
> —Psalm 119:30 NASB

I think it's safe to say society usually tries to do what is right, just, and fair. Unfortunately, society measures these concepts with a cultural compass—one that is attracted to the constant changing and shifting ideas and ideals driven by Hollywood and mainstream media.

We, as a nation, have lost our true north. So how do we get it back?

Cristen says that nature shows us the way. An amateur astrologist would use the stars, while the hiker may align his or her analogous (not digital) watch with the sun. No watch? Make a sundial. You could also look for moss, which is thicker on the south or southeastern side of a tree. But the easiest way is to use a GPS.

Most GPS devices today have a true north setting. Punch in your location and let the computer do the rest.

God is a good god. He doesn't leave us to rely on omens and signs. We don't have to scour the heavens or decipher dreams. He inspired forty different authors from three different continents over a span of more than 1,500 years to give us the perfect GPS.

The Bible is "God's Positioning System."

If our destination is heaven, then the Bible is our true north.

> There is a path before each person that seems right, but
> it ends in death.

> —Proverbs 14:12 NLT

Without the Bible as our authority, we wander off course. Without true north, precious life created by God falls prey to a woman's choice. Without true north, institutions created and defined by God are redefined by the vocal minority. Without true north, chastity until marriage is mocked, modesty is unheard of, and debauchery is celebrated.

Just like the Bible says it will be:

> You should know this, Timothy, that in the last days there will be very difficult times. For people will love only themselves and their money. They will be boastful and proud, scoffing at God, disobedient to their parents, and ungrateful. They will consider nothing sacred. They will be unloving and unforgiving; they will slander others and have no self-control. They will be cruel and hate what is good. They will betray their friends, be reckless, be puffed up with pride, and love pleasure rather than God. They will act religious, but they will reject the power that could make them godly. Stay away from people like that!

> —2 Timothy 3:1–5 NLT

Living by the magnetic compass—succumbing to the magnetic pull of society—is the easy way. The path is wide and paved with good intentions, but it is the sure path of destruction. Many a sailor has found himself miles off course without true north. Oh, that it were only a ship at stake.

Jesus has a better way.

His way leads to peace. His way leads to rest. His way leads to the soul-satisfaction of living for something greater than yourself. His way leads to a mansion tailor-made for you. It is filled with treasure that moths cannot eat and thieves cannot steal. The way of Christ leads to garments of salvation, robes of righteousness, and crowns of glory. It leads to a banquet with the best food and the choicest wine.

Don't follow the crowd. Activate your GPS. Punch in your location. Surrender your imperfect plans to His perfect will and follow His lead. Stand strong. Don't back down. Love in the midst of hate. Lift your hands and raise your voice.

Shine.

> Before I was afflicted I went astray, but now I keep Your word. You are good and do good; teach me Your statutes.
>
> —Psalm 119:67–68 NASB

THE FLAT TIRE

Make my steps steady through Your promise; don't let
any sin dominate me.

—Psalm 119:133 HCSB

Question: When is a flat tire a fabulous thing?
Answer: When it is an answered prayer.

I am a frustrated seminary student. No, I am not attending seminary,
but I want to. In fact, I want to so much that I can almost taste it.
Assuming, of course, that seminary has a taste. That's weird. Never
mind. Indulge me a moment while I explain.

Jesus has changed my life. Sometimes I wonder if my high school
and college friends would even recognize me. Sometimes I hardly
recognize myself. Don't get me wrong, I have been a Bible-reading
churchgoer most of my life, but that did not stop a decade-long rebellious
streak.

In 2000, I experienced an awakening. For reasons I can't explain,
God touched my heart, and I wanted Him in my life. I found a large,
dynamic church that taught the Bible boldly. I joined my first Bible
study and sat wide-eyed and open-mouthed as a blond Southern belle
named Beth Moore opened up Scripture in a way that turned words on
a page into a 3-D Technicolor adventure.

Soon, sermons and Bible studies weren't enough. I wanted to
understand the context of the times in which Jesus lived. What was
Ephesus like? What were the Romans like? What was the mood of the
Jews as a nation when Christ arrived on the scene? Where could I go

to find the original meaning of the original language of the original manuscripts so that I could further study for myself?

A mentor suggested seminary, and that was all it took. I didn't need to pray, and I didn't need to think about it; the matter was settled, and I was going.

Or was I?

> Don't brag about tomorrow, since you don't know what
> the day will bring.
>
> —Proverbs 27:1 NLT

I hunted down my college transcripts. I coerced my pastor and colleagues to write letters of recommendation. I gathered my courage and applied.

"Okay, Lord," I prayed, "if this is of You, I will get accepted."

To my surprise, my acceptance letter brought anxiety instead of excitement. After praying about it a while, I decided to wait so that my husband and I could save our money and pay the tuition out of pocket.

At the end of my deferment, I let the application drop.

Months later, I reapplied. I got the acceptance letter a few days later, telling me that I could enroll in one month.

On the last day of the month with a few hours to go, I sat in front of my computer, not moving. I saw the class I wanted to take. The money was in our account. Nothing was stopping me. After a few minutes, I turned off the computer and went to bed. I let my enrollment drop for the second time.

Three months later, I was half surfing the web and half watching TV with my husband when a familiar ding alerted me to a new e-mail.

It was a notification from Dallas Theological Seminary that their Lay Institute was gearing up for another round of classes. Immediately, I perked up. Lay Institute! Maybe this was what I was supposed to do. Maybe God didn't want me in seminary, but that didn't mean He wanted me to forgo further education, right?

I spent the rest of the evening reading class descriptions, and by the time I'd finished, I knew this was right. I got Mike's blessing and signed up.

The closer I got to the start date, the more uneasy I became. I had asked Mike to bless it, but had I asked God? I felt a surge of anxiety when I looked at my calendar. I was getting ready to teach one Bible study and start writing another. I had between four and six separate speaking engagements a month for the next three months, and unless I wanted to take precious time away from my family, there was no way school was feasible.

I withdrew from the roster.

Fast forward to the end of the semester—the familiar spiritual itch was back. Once again, I had a full calendar, but I signed up for two classes anyway. Since the desire would not go away, it was clearly what God wanted me to do, right?

I suppose God would have answered that question had I asked Him properly.

You see, sometimes when we really want something, we tend to pray a one-sided prayer. We ask God to clarify His will, then we try to mold His will into ours. We don't stop to silently listen. We don't wait on Him. We don't ask Him to speak clearly to us because, at the end of the day, we aren't asking Him what we *should* do. We are asking Him to bless what we have *already decided* to do.

The first day of class arrived. Since the school is approximately forty-five minutes away and I would be driving during rush hour, Mike came home early so I could find my way around campus. As he bounded through the door, he beamed at me and said, "So, babe, are you excited?"

I was anything but.

Caitlyn was exhausted and didn't want me to leave. Nick was unusually clingy too. I turned to my husband.

"What am I doing?" I asked. "I am a mom. I am a wife. I have a busy calendar. This cannot be what God wants me to do."

My husband was clearly fed up with my inability to commit to something I'd been talking about for over a year.

"No," he said firmly. "You are not going to let the kids do this to you. You want to do this. I want you to do this. I've got everything under control here, so go!"

I left.

The farther I got from my house, the worse I felt. The cluster of butterflies fluttering around my stomach had morphed into an angry colony of bats, wildly beating their way into my chest. As I turned south on the interstate, I felt a lump in my throat. My heart raced as though I'd just finished a hundred-yard dash.

"Okay, God," I prayed out loud. "You have got my attention. If You don't want me to go, I won't go. But You have to stop me because I am going to these classes to find You! I want to know You; I want to learn about You and teach others about You!"

You know what happened next, don't you?

I got a flat tire.

I got the biggest, flattest, most glorious, divinely deflated tire you could imagine. At first, I wasn't sure; perhaps my car was off balance. Then I felt the wheel pull gently to the right. I looked at the indicator on my dash board. Sure enough, that tire was flat.

I was elated. "Really, God?" I shrieked, "You really don't want me to go to seminary? You would really answer me like that?"

I stopped on the shoulder and looked around. Had I scoured a map for the safest spot to pull over, I would have picked right where I was: a long stretch where an entrance ramp converged into an exit ramp, a full lane over from the southbound traffic speeding by.

I threw my head back and laughed at the ridiculousness of it. Then I called my husband.

His phone was off. He *never* turns his phone off.

Remembering that he'd gone to the gym, I called Lifetime Fitness, asking them to page Mike Carrell for an emergency. No luck. When I reached him an hour later, he apologized, insisting that he never heard his name over the loudspeaker.

Of course he didn't. If he had, he would've rushed to my aid, given me his car, and waited for help while I drove to seminary. But God didn't want me to go to seminary.

He wanted me back in radio. *Christian* radio.

> But if any of you lacks wisdom, let him ask of God, who gives to all generously and without reproach, and it will be given to him. But he must ask in faith without any doubting, for the one who doubts is like the surf of the sea, driven and tossed by the wind.
>
> —James 1:5–6 NASB

I still have to remind myself that the most important part of prayer is listening. If I don't have an immediate answer, that usually means wait for further instructions. God is not a god of confusion. He doesn't play games or give mixed signals. He spoke through the prophets, sent His Son, and speaks through the Bible and His Spirit. He wants us to know Him. He is never too busy for us, and we are always on the top of His priority list.

He wants to talk to you. Right now, right where you are. Don't put Him off. Do not ignore His whisper. One way or another, He will get your attention, even if it takes a flat tire.

CHRISTIAN MCNUGGETS

How sweet are Your words to my taste! Yes, sweeter
than honey to my mouth!

—Psalm 119:103 NASB

I owe my newfound interest in "clean eating" to my friend Casey Eden
Sollock. Until I met Casey, I thought I was doing pretty well in the
nutrition department. I favored low-calorie snacks like pretzels, rice
cakes, and crackers, enjoying every bite of the thiamine mononitrate,
calcium chloride, and disodium EDTA blend. I drank my diet soda
by the liter, naively savoring each ounce of caramel color expertly
combined with the perfect blend of aspertain and phosperic acid. I doled
out all kinds of processed, packaged goodies to my children, smugly
congratulating myself on their low-fat diet.

And then I met Casey.

Oy.

Casey suggested, rather insisted, that I watch the documentary
Food, Inc. Highly disturbing, yes. Menu altering, not really (we already
bought organic meat).

Next on her list was *Forks over Knives*. To my husband's dismay,
this was decisively more effective. I spent four days experimenting with
new recipes like raw vegan Baja veggie wraps and silken tofu with sun-
dried tomatoes. Looking for new and exciting ways to serve bean curd
grew tiresome, so I gave up. Remembering that God gave us meat to
eat, I relaxed a bit and, instead, concentrated on slowly removing the
processed foods from our pantry.

Casey, sensing that I had not quite crossed over to her side, sent me the link for *Hungry for a Change*. I watched it, not necessarily willingly, from start to finish.

Stick a fork in me, friends. I'm done.

According to Dr. Alejandro Junger, "We are not eating food anymore. We are eating food-like products, and they are adorned. They are made to look better and smell better so that people are attracted to them." We are eating things that don't exist in nature; things concocted by chemists, not chefs.

In a nutshell, we're eating more food than ever before, yet finding ourselves increasingly malnourished. We consume highly sweetened products that are rich in calories, but nutrionally void. Statistically, over 30% of American adults are obese, but starving on a cellular level.

Of course, this isn't really a story about food. It just makes a good spiritual parallel.

> Like newborn babies, you must crave pure spiritual milk
> so that you will grow into a full experience of salvation.
> Cry out for this nourishment, now that you have had a
> taste of the Lord's kindness.
>
> —1 Peter 2:2–3 NLT

Are you drinking pure, spiritual milk or living on small portions of Christian McNuggets?

In my postcollege, premarriage era, I had no reason to be depressed. I had a fun job and good friends (actually, friend-like products, but that's another story for another time). One of those friends had a boat, and we spent many Saturdays on the lake, enjoying a full cooler and good company.

Although summer Saturdays would bleed into Sunday, I rarely missed church. A friend and I would meet, bleary-eyed and disheveled, at Starbucks. There, we would caffeinate and recap what we remembered from the previous day as we carpooled to the service.

We would sing to the music and nod to the message. Since neither of us had boyfriends, we might visit the single's class following worship.

After church, we would typically land on a patio somewhere, nursing our headaches with more headache-inducing drinks.

That was my spiritual nourishment for the week. Aside from chatting with God briefly during the day or praying as I drifted off to sleep, that was all the soul sustenance I got.

No wonder I felt empty.

I used to watch other Christians interact with each other, questioning the sincerity of their peace. Even when they had problems, they seemed joyful. I knew how to play the game, but these people seemed to mean it. Somehow, they had tapped into something I had not discovered, and I wanted what they had.

I started attending Bible studies. The daily homework and weekly accountability made a big difference, at least during the study. Once it stopped, so did the warm sense of the Holy Spirit.

I tried listening to Christian music. I subscribed to a Christian devotional. I read Max Lucado and Beth Moore, always with the same results: short bursts of inspiration followed by emptiness and depression.

What was I doing wrong?

I wasn't drinking the living water, nor was I consuming heart-healthy spiritual meals. I was surviving on Christian McNuggets.

> You satisfy me as with rich food; my mouth will praise
> You with joyful lips.
>
> —Psalm 63:5 HCSB

Church is essential. We are called as members of the body of Christ to meet together weekly for worship and instruction. We can grab daily devotions to go and get bite-sized portions of Scripture. Christian books offer comfort through real-life testimonies. They provide guidance and wisdom and can open our hearts and eyes to see things differently. These are all good things, but they are vitamins nonetheless—meant to be used as supplements, not daily bread.

The real meat—the life-giving, soul-saving sustenance—comes from a personal relationship with Jesus Christ developed by studying

His Word. Nothing else will do, and nothing can take its place. You don't need more religion or religious activities. Christianity isn't about religion. It's about a relationship.

It's about Jesus and you. No fancy packaging and no processing. No flavor-enhancing nonsense and no misleading marketing.

He is the King of Kings, Lord of Lords, and the Creator of heaven and earth, and He makes Himself available to you. He works with your schedule; He meets on your terms.

With Jesus, there is no need for portion control. You can supersize Him all you want because the more Christ you get, the more you'll want. Before you know it, you will bear the fruit of your new, spiritually healthy lifestyle. You'll have more faith to flex. Old habits will melt away and be replaced with kindness, gentleness, love, peace, perseverance, and joy.

You will experience true joy in spite of your circumstances. You will go from tolerating unpleasant people to loving them. Yes, I'm serious. You will love them with the love of Christ, poured into you by God Himself. He'll correct your spiritual nearsightedness, and you'll see things through the lens of eternity. Trials and storms will start to make sense, but when they don't, you will rest in the knowledge that "God works all things for the good of those who love Him and are called according to His purposes" (Rom. 8:28).

Your life will have purpose. Where you once coasted aimlessly, you'll begin to live intentionally. You will do more than you dreamed you could do, for when you operate in the power of Christ, there are no limits.

And you will have peace.

Come to the table. Even now, He beckons you. Take time every day to focus on Him in silence. Ask Him what He wants to say to you. Don't read through Scripture quickly as a duty, but chew on every Spirit-inspired word. Enjoy it. Meditate on it, process it, and move on to the next bite.

The table is set. The feast is ready. And you, friend, are His guest of honor.

Your words were found and I ate them, And Your words became for me a joy and the delight of my heart; For I have been called by Your name, O Lord God of hosts.

—Jeremiah 15:16 NASB

BIG-BOY BED

A woman suffering from bleeding for twelve years, who had spent all she had on doctors yet could not be healed by any, approached from behind and touched the tassel of His robe. Instantly her bleeding stopped.

—Luke 8:43–44 HCSB

A mile marker for me in child rearing was becoming a crib-free mom. I remember the Sunday it became a reality: I took the kids to my parents' house for the afternoon while Mike and my mother-in-law put Nick's new bedroom together. By the time we got home, he was the proud owner of a big-boy bed, complete with new bedding, a dresser, and a stepping stool. I will never forget the look on his face when he when saw his "new" room.

That night, instead of putting up the usual resistance, our son clambered under the covers as fast as he could. Bedtime is important in our house, and Mike and I deliberately stretch our "good nights" with the children. This is when they open up, talking about their day and anything else on their little minds. I'll climb into Caitlyn's bed, hold her in my arms, and listen. Then we say our prayers, and Mike and I switch. He'll say good night to Caitlyn while I spend time with Nick.

With Nick, it hadn't been the same bonding experience. I'd sit on the floor by his converted crib, asking questions. Then prayers, one last sip of water, and a kiss good night.

With the new bed in place, that changed.

I climbed into bed and pulled him close, breathing in the sweet scent of his shampoo. I kissed his chubby cheek and held his plump little hand.

"What was the best part of your day, Nicky?" Our conversation was precious.

It struck me as I left his room—the crib had been a barrier. It put a physical wall between me and my son. Once we removed it, I could get closer, both physically and emotionally.

Do you have any "cribs" in your life? What barriers might there be between you and Jesus?

In the eighth chapter of Luke, we learn about a woman with a physical barrier. She had been bleeding for twelve years, most likely with a menstrual issue. Scripture does not specify whether or not the woman was a Gentile, but if she was Jewish, this was a very real problem.

According to Jewish law, the bleeding made her ceremoniously unclean. Men were not allowed to touch women during their cycle nor were they allowed to handle anything that the woman had touched. Women were not declared "clean" until seven days after their cycle ended. This woman had possibly gone without physical contact for twelve years.

> "Who touched Me?" Jesus asked. When they all denied it, Peter said, "Master, the crowds are hemming You in and pressing against You."
>
> "Someone did touch Me," said Jesus. "I know that power has gone out from Me." When the woman saw that she was discovered, she came trembling and fell down before Him.
>
> —Luke 8:45–47a HCSB

What was that moment like?

I picture Christ turning and scanning the crowd. Horrified, the woman's eyes dart wildly around, looking for an escape route. Finding none, she looks desperately at Jesus, then at the ground.

She glances up again, and her heart drops to her stomach. As Jesus looks through her eyes and into her soul, her resolve fades away. She falls to her knees and confesses.

> In the presence of all the people, she declared the reason
> she had touched Him and how she was instantly cured.
>
> —Luke 8:47b HCSB

The whole crowd watched and listened to her humiliation, her secret, and her shame. Imagine them leaning in with eager anticipation to see what Jesus would do. Would He yell? Would He demand that she be turned over to the Pharisees? Would He banish her from the community?

> "Daughter," he said to her, "your faith has made you
> well. Go in peace."
>
> —Luke 8:48 NLT

Jesus called her "daughter." He praised her faith. He released her to go in peace. How I wish we could hear the tone of His voice and see the look in His eyes. Do you think the woman walked calmly back to her family or raced off like a child? I can almost hear her, excitedly tripping over her words as she relayed how the *rabboni* had demolished the twelve-year-old barrier that stood between her and the world.

Jesus came to bulldoze the walls and barriers that keep us from intimacy with Himself and with others. What is the crib that keeps you from Him? What is stealing your peace? Is it insecurity? Anxiety? Financial fear? Busyness? An unhealthy habit or addiction? Jesus beckons you to set it down. He can obliterate those strongholds. Your "big-boy bed" is ready, and He is waiting to hold you close and set you free.

> You were cleansed from your sins when you obeyed the
> truth, so now you must show sincere love to each other
> as brothers and sisters. Love each other deeply with all

your heart. For you have been born again, but not to a life that will quickly end. Your new life will last forever because it comes from the eternal, living word of God.

—1 Peter 4:7–8 NLT

THE PIGGY BANK

We are pressed on every side by troubles, but we are not crushed. We are perplexed, but not driven to despair. We are hunted down, but never abandoned by God. We get knocked down, but we are not destroyed.

—2 Corinthians 4:8–9 NLT

My husband is the ultimate "Mr. Fix-It."

In fact, when something breaks, the kids and I have a saying: "That's okay! Daddy can fix *anything*!"

We once really put his expertise to the test.

When my daughter was born, a dear friend of mine gave her a beautiful porcelain piggy bank. It decoratively adorned a shelf in her bedroom, sitting in quiet but empty anticipation until Caitlyn turned three. Then Mike and I started giving her spare change anytime she did a small chore.

She loved the merry sound of quarters, dimes, and nickels clinking on the bottom of the bank as she dropped them in. That little piggy bank was quickly elevated to a prized and cherished possession, and to my delight, Caitlyn started looking for chores.

The emptying ritual is done on the kitchen table, and afterward, the piggy bank is to be immediately returned to its spot on the shelf. But one time, it wasn't.

On that fateful day, Caitlyn left it on the stairs. About two warnings and an hour later, she accidently kicked it all the way to the bottom where it shattered on the hardwood floors. Her shriek broke my heart.

She sobbed uncontrollably in my arms for about ten minutes. Sweet little Nick kept trying to tell her it was okay, but she knew otherwise.

"It's in too many pieces, Mommy! Daddy can't fix it!" I didn't vocalize it, but inwardly, I agreed.

At the sound of the garage door, my daughter raced to meet Daddy, tears streaming down her face. Mike did the sweetest, most tender thing he could've done. He held her, told her he loved her, and wiped away her tears. Then he looked through the broken pieces and gave her cautious hope.

Later that night, I came downstairs to see my husband deliberately, painstakingly putting the shattered piggy bank back together—bit by bit and piece by piece— holding it carefully in his hands to make sure the glue adhered before adding another fragment. He worked slowly and methodically until it was completed.

It was good as new, save the cracks.

I think the experience resonated with me so deeply because I identify with the poor little piggy bank. I, too, have sat amidst the broken pieces of my life, wondering how it could ever come together, too blinded by sorrow and pain to see that there was anything left to salvage. And just like Mike with Caitlyn, Jesus wiped away my tears, gave me hope, and carefully put me back together.

I was good as new, save the scars.

My daughter has outgrown the piggy bank, but not me. I treasure her little porcelain pig, not in spite of the cracks but because of them.

I find strength in my scars. And although I'm sure my daughter wishes she'd never broken that piggy bank, I see it as a beautiful illustration of God's love at work in our lives.

Is your life in pieces? Take heart, sweet friend. Your heavenly Father can fix *anything*.

> He sent His word and healed them; He rescued them from the Pit.

> —Psalm 107:20 HCSB

FIRST DAY OF KINDERGARTEN

I consider that our present sufferings are not worth comparing with the glory that will be revealed in us.

—Romans 8:18 NIV

Where has the time gone? I now have two kids in elementary school. If I close my eyes, I can still see them as babies. I recently found a picture of my daughter on her first day of kindergarten. Feeling nostalgic, I went to my journal and flipped back to August 2011. There was no entry on her first day of school, but I'd written this a week earlier:

> I woke up this morning to find my sweet daughter curled up against me in bed. As I smoothed her tousled hair and kissed her rosy cheek, I marveled at the fact that she is five years old and starting kindergarten in less than a week. Even though my children are four and five, I still sometimes feel like a rookie in the mom department.
>
> Caitlyn and I are both anticipating this day; she eagerly, me anxiously. Since leaving my full-time job in radio this year (2011), it has been just me and the kids every day. With day care no longer an option, we're a package deal. They come with me when I buy groceries, when I see the doctor, and when I go for a jog. Parks are cheaper than movies, so we've put serious mileage on the jogger stroller. It is time for her to start school, and she and I are both ready. But I will miss my little girl.

Caitlyn, on the other hand, has been counting down the days all summer. Yesterday, I heard her bare feet patter downstairs an hour and fifteen minutes earlier than usual because she wanted to "practice getting ready." We sat at the breakfast table, she sipping orange juice and me with my coffee, talking softly about all things school.

I remember that conversation like it happened this morning.

"Are you excited, honey?" I asked.

"Mm hmm," came her sleepy reply. Then, catching me off guard, she continued, "And nervous. Were you nervous, mommy?"

I have a policy with my children: be honest.

I racked my brain, trying to find that decades-old memory. I have a vapor of an image of climbing onto a bus with my backpack. I recall a later year, trying to fall asleep in our New Brighton, Minnesota home, new outfit laid out on my dresser, tossing and turning long before sleep claimed me. But kindergarten?

Nope. Nothing.

"Sweetie, I'm sure I was a little nervous. But here is what I can tell you. I loved elementary school, and you will too. You'll meet so many new friends and learn lots of exciting things. You have nothing to be nervous about."

That conversation has replayed in my mind more than once over the years. Kindergarten was such a monumental event for both of my children. At one point, it had been the same for me, and I can't remember a thing about it. In fact, I can't remember the "firsts" of any elementary school days, save the fourth grade, when we'd moved from Minnesota to Overland Park, Kansas. I wore a pink dress my grandmother made, and the teacher had us move our desks in a circle.

When you think about it, in the grand scheme of eternity, our entire earthly lives are like the first day of kindergarten.

For our present troubles are small and won't last very long. Yet they produce for us a glory that vastly outweighs them and will last forever!

—2 Corinthians 4:17 NLT

Let's not take anything away from our troubles. I know women who are, right now, going through the heartbreak of infertility and the devastation of miscarriage after miscarriage. As I type, a friend is incapacitated from back and neck pain. I am petitioning God on behalf of a family member because of a spot on his lung. Also on my prayer list is a woman picking up the pieces of her life after losing both her job and her husband. People are suffering all across the globe.

The apostle Paul knew suffering. In his second letter to the church in Corinth, he wrote,

> I have worked harder, been put in prison more often, been whipped times without number, and faced death again and again. Five different times the Jewish leaders gave me thirty-nine lashes. Three times I was beaten with rods. Once I was stoned. Three times I was shipwrecked. Once I spent a whole night and a day adrift at sea. I have worked hard and long, enduring many sleepless nights. I have been hungry and thirsty and have often gone without food. I have shivered in the cold, without enough clothing to keep me warm (2 Corinthians 11:23–25, 27 NLT).

And Paul, the great apostle, author of thirteen books in our New Testament, the one who saw the glory of Christ on the road to Damascus, the one taken up in a vision to the third heaven, says that in comparison to the glory we have coming, these trials and troubles *aren't even worth counting.*

Oh, that we would live with the perspective of Paul.

> Since you have been raised to new life with Christ, set your sights on the realities of heaven, where Christ sits in the place of honor at God's right hand. Think about the things of heaven, not the things of earth.

—Colossians 3:1–2 NLT

Your very peace of mind, your very joy, hinges on your thoughts. What are you dwelling on? The troubles surrounding you or the glory awaiting you? Wherever you are in life, there is more. Let the truth of that statement permeate your every waking moment. Let it direct your words and actions. Let it affect your generosity, your service, your worship, your church attendance, and your prayers. Let the reality of Christ and His coming kingdom flood your soul.

He is real, He loves you, and He is preparing a place for you even now.

> Do not let your hearts be troubled. You believe in God;
> believe also in me. My Father's house has many rooms;
> if that were not so, would I have told you that I am going
> there to prepare a place for you?

—John 14:1–2 NASB

THE ARGUMENT

> God saved you by his grace when you believed. And you
> can't take credit for this; it is a gift from God. Salvation
> is not a reward for the good things we have done, so
> none of us can boast about it.
>
> —Ephesians 2:8–9 NLT

Out of all of God's attributes, I struggle the most with grace.

How ironic. The very thing that saves and justifies me is the very thing I am so inclined to reject.

Perhaps it is because I am keenly aware that I do not deserve it.

I can walk the Christian walk and speak the Christian talk. I can give the proper churchy response and tell you "what Jesus would do," but if I were completely transparent, I would confess that I blow it more often than not, and my capacity for sin is greater than my capacity to love.

So is yours.

Ouch! I know that hurts. I wish I could soften it. However, there is a measure of freedom to be found when we can admit that our motives are not completely pure. We are not completely honest. We are far from who we want to be.

We hate to admit it, don't we? Some of us never do. The apostle Paul did, and my hypocritical heart is thankful.

> The sinful nature wants to do evil, which is just the
> opposite of what the Spirit wants. And the Spirit gives
> us desires that are the opposite of what the sinful

nature desires. These two forces are constantly fighting each other, so you are not free to carry out your good intentions.

—Galatians 5:17 NLT

I have a forty five–minute commute to work. I either use that time to pray or listen to worship music and sermons. One morning, I spent it arguing with God. The subject? Grace.

I had plans with a friend I wanted to break. I had offered to bring a meal to a sick friend and was scouring my mind for plausible excuses not to. I was exhausted, grumpy, and in no mood for the heavy conviction plaguing my heart.

Knowing that I would not break my commitments, I sank further into my foul mood. Echoes of a recent teaching on grace played on repeat in my mind: "Grace doesn't force you to obey. Grace frees you to live a life of joyful obedience."

I was not feeling free. I had no desire whatsoever to joyfully serve my friends, but I was dead set on begrudgingly doing it out of guilt. On top of that, I was angry at God for expecting me to joyfully obey.

The Lord must have been lovingly shaking His head.

I was frustrated that I had made plans. I was irritated that I was frustrated, and I was completely missing the point of grace.

Just as a father has compassion on his children, so the Lord has compassion on those who fear Him. For He Himself knows our frame; He is mindful that we are but dust.

—Psalm 103:13–14 NASB

Out loud, I cried, "Well, explain it to me then! I don't feel like joyfully obeying You! So does that mean I just cancel my plans and sulk?"

Out of the blue, He brought Caitlyn and Nick to mind.

"How do you see your children?" He asked.

I see them as perfect. My children are absolutely perfect, and there is not one thing about them I would change.

But here's the deal, they are not perfect.

Caitlyn has been known to cheat at Candyland. Nick still has tantrums. They fight like cats and dogs. They misbehave, "forget" to make their beds and brush their teeth, and complain about eating their vegetables. I am constantly reminding them to say "please" and "thank you," and even find myself saying things like, "That's it! You're not allowed to look at each other while we're in the car" (another story for another time).

But that's not what I see when I look at them.

I see perfection, not because of what they do, but because of who they are.

They are mine, and their behavior has no bearing on that. I don't love them more when they get along, and I don't love them less when they act out. My children have no power to affect my level of love for them. They can receive it or refuse it, but they cannot change it. They have my absolute favor simply because they're mine.

That's what grace is. Favor. Unmerited, undeserved, pure, and absolute favor.

Because of that favor, God delights in you, whether you joyfully obey or purposefully don't. You can't earn more of His favor, and you can't lose it. You can't impress Him or disappoint Him. Your thoughts don't shock Him, your grumpiness doesn't frustrate Him, and your begrudging service doesn't upset Him.

I wrestle with this because I know God is a perfectionist, and He is. He is a holy, mighty God, and a holy God cannot tolerate sin. How unfathomable it is then that the God who must punish sin *became* sin and absorbed His own wrath on the cross.

If you are in Christ, your Father sees you as perfect, not because of what you do, but because of who you are.

You are His, and because of that, you cannot escape His love. You are under His favor. You are the recipient of inexhaustible grace. You are accepted, forgiven, redeemed, chosen, cherished, and honored.

Meditate on that. Swim in it. Drink it in. Wear it like a robe and own it.

You are His, and He has set you free, not to do whatever you want because that enslaves us to our selfish desires. Christ has set us free to do what was previously impossible. Through His Spirit, we are free to live generously. We can love sacrificially. We can serve selflessly, not in our strength, but His.

We are free to joyfully obey, and this is what I discovered that morning: if I am faithful to do what God asks of me, the joy will follow.

I went to lunch with my friend that day, and was strengthened and encouraged by her friendship. Afterward, Caitlyn and I together made the meal and delivered it. What had looked like a burden became a blessing. And by the way, the next time you are tempted to argue with God, remember this—He always wins.

We praise You, Father, for all that You are.

> My soul, praise the Lord, and do not forget all His benefits. He forgives all your sin; He heals all your diseases. He redeems your life from the Pit; He crowns you with faithful love and compassion. He satisfies you with goodness; your youth is renewed like the eagle.
>
> —Psalm 103:2–5 HCSB

SNOW DAZE

The Lord is my light and my salvation—so why should I be afraid? The Lord is my fortress, protecting me from danger, so why should I tremble?

—Psalm 27:1 NLT

Until 1998, my entire life had been spent in different states with one thing in common: they each had four separate seasons. Texas has two: summer and a short burst of fall-winter-spring all rolled into one. Sunblock is to a Texan what an ice scraper is to a Minnesotan – essential.

Why is that relevant? Because growing up in the North and Midwest, I learned how to drive on ice and snow. Living in Texas, I am in the vast minority.

When snow hits Texas, Texas closes. One inch in the forecast? Cities shut down. School is called off before the first flake hits the ground. Things like water, flashlights, and duct tape sell out. The masses panic while transplants like me shake their heads and grin. It takes more than an inch or two to scare us.

To be fair, driving in treacherous conditions is easier when you live in a city built for winter. Dallas/Fort Worth has approximately fourteen snowplows (just a guess). Minneapolis, where I got my learner's permit, has about fourteen per neighborhood. In Colorado, where I passed my driver's test, sleet and snow aren't "arctic blasts" or "snow events;" they are just a normal part of the forecast.

When you learn to drive on slick roads, you pick up the essentials quickly. Here are a few:

- Drive slowly.
- Be prepared (flashlights, ice scrapers, blankets, etc.).
- Be aware of other drivers.
- Avoid dangerous situations (main roads over side or back roads).
- When you skid or slide (when, not if) don't slam on the brakes. Let go of the wheel and trust the car to right itself.

Drivers in the north know you have little control on ice. Solomon knew we have even less in life:

> Enjoy prosperity while you can. But when hard times strike, realize that both come from God. That way you will realize that nothing is certain in this life.
>
> —Ecclesiastes 7:14 NLT

Jerry Jones, owner of the Dallas Cowboys, knows this too.

Jones planned for years to build a palace of a stadium that could house the crown jewel of the NFL—the Super Bowl. I first saw the stadium plans in 2001 while visiting Valley Ranch. On May 27, 2009, the dream came to fruition, and the DFW area came together in a Super Bowl campaign that made the presidential race look tame.

Two years later, Jones got the main event, and North Texas got walloped with an unprecedented ice storm. The metroplex watched as plans and revenue slipped down the drain.

> In everything we do, we show that we are true ministers of God. We patiently endure troubles and hardships and calamities of every kind.
>
> —2 Corinthians 6:4 NLT

If I might paraphrase Paul's words to the Corinthians, the forecast calls for ice and snow. Maybe not today and maybe not tomorrow, but at some point in life, we can count on this: The ground underneath us will shake.

Upon what have you built your foundation?

Whether on land or in life, the advice for treacherous conditions remains the same.

- *Drive slowly.* Don't make rushed decisions. Get sound counsel before making big moves, and always seek the Lord in prayer. My husband has a firm policy: always wait 24 hours before answering. No one will mind if you say you need to think about it.
- *Be prepared.* Many of life's biggest pitfalls can be softened by responsible living. Don't rack up debt by spending what you don't have. Live beneath your means. Don't smoke. Don't eat only processed food. Incorporate exercise into your daily routine. Know who your children run around with. Know what they read and what they watch.
- *Be aware of the other drivers.* Be wary of unhealthy influences. Make sure you have fellowship with other believers.
- *Avoid dangerous situations.* Know your areas of temptation or weakness, and stay away from them. Don't assume that you're strong enough to resist.
- *Let go of the wheel.* Remember that control is an illusion. Remember also that nothing reaches you before first passing through your Father's hands. When the ground is shaking beneath you, rest in the knowledge that God is for you. He loves you, and He causes all things to work for your good and His glory. He alone knows the plans He has for you, and He alone holds the map.

Teach me Your way, O Lord; I will walk in Your truth;
Unite my heart to fear Your name.

—Psalm 86:11 NASB

THE PLATE

But as for you, Israel my servant, Jacob my chosen one, descended from Abraham my friend, I have called you back from the ends of the earth, saying, "You are my servant." For I have chosen you and will not throw you away.

—Isaiah 41:8–9 NLT

I have discovered something about myself: I operate best with a bit too much on my plate.

While I am not a workaholic, I am most certainly a worker bee. I got my first job at fifteen. Before that, I babysat. Before I was old enough to babysit, I dragged my dad's snow shovel up and down the block, offering to clear neighbors' driveways for two bucks a pop. During the spring and summer months, I would corral the neighborhood kids and produce musicals and talent shows. My mother loves to tell the story of the language I wrote in my second-grade social studies class, and the consequent "F" I received because of it (honestly— the teacher should've cut me some slack. I was writing a new language!).

I am happier with a full plate, and chances are, so are you. No one does well with too much spare time.

There is a reason for that, and it's this: God made you for a purpose, and He has specifically and uniquely gifted you to carry it out.

I can't tell you what your gift is, but I *can* tell you what your purpose is. It's not a secret. You don't need a spiritual experience to discover it, and you don't need to meditate or achieve nirvana to understand it. In fact, your purpose is the same as mine.

You and I are called to the real estate business. If we had spiritual business cards, they would read "Kingdom Expansion Agent." We are also in the party business. Our job is simple. Go to the ends of the earth and pass out invitations.

Our purpose and reason for existing is to bring glory to God and to build up His church. God, in His grace and goodness, has made this the key to the fulfillment of our joy.

> We have different gifts, according to the grace given to each of us. If your gift is prophesying, then prophesy in accordance with your faith; if it is serving, then serve; if it is teaching, then teach; if it is to encourage, then give encouragement; if it is giving, then give generously; if it is to lead, do it diligently; if it is to show mercy, do it cheerfully.

—Romans 12:6–8 NIV

Too many people in the body of Christ drift from activity to activity, piling one thing after another on their plate, always fighting off mild frustration. Too many churches plug people into ministries outside of their area of gifting, then wonder why they can't get volunteers to stick around. Perhaps you didn't know you had a spiritual gift. Perhaps you've heard about them, but you have never explored it. Here are three reasons why you should:

You have an innate need to be needed. Don't cringe. God made you this way. This only becomes a problem when the need is misplaced. This is why so many women suffer from "empty nest syndrome" when their last baby flies the coop. The fact is that God made you with more in mind. Your plate should never be empty. Your specific skill set has been divinely designed to fulfill a specific job in the body of Christ, and you are needed.

It will satisfy the longing in your heart. A Maserati was created for speed. A racehorse was groomed from birth to race. You were created to bring glory to Christ. Trying to find purpose outside of God's plan for your life is fruitless and frustrating. More money won't make you happy when the money you have can't scratch the itch. The skin of a twenty-year-old didn't give you peace as a twenty-year-old, and it won't give you peace now—neither will more clothes, more cars, or more toys. You are a puzzle piece looking for your place, and once you start working in your area of gifting, you'll feel the "click."

God's plan for you is better than your plan for you. Years ago, I was living in Kansas City, miserable and in an emotionally unhealthy relationship. My bachelor's degree in broadcast journalism sat, gathering dust, on a shelf. I cried out to God for help and instead of fixing my current circumstances, He changed them with a set of marching orders: "Go to Texas." So with a broken heart and shattered dreams, I obeyed. Then He put me in radio. Then He gave me a marriage. Then He gave me a ministry and a message, and *joy* along with it. For once, my plate was full of the right things.

> Now all glory to God, who is able, through his mighty power at work within us, to accomplish infinitely more than we might ask or think.
>
> —Ephesians 3:20 NLT

Do you long to be part of something bigger? Do you wonder why peace is elusive? Why settle for fleeting happiness when God offers lasting joy?

The first step to discovering your spiritual gift is to ask God what it is. Pray about it every day for thirty days. You may think that you know what it is, but ask someone you trust what *he or she* thinks. Find an online spiritual gifts test and take it.

Next, ask God what you should do. Consider making an appointment with your pastor to ask about serving in the area of your gifting. If you haven't already, plug into a community of believers. Make knowing Jesus your priority because, my friend, you are certainly His priority, and He has a plan for your life. He will do things through you that your mind cannot conceive.

You will go from merely existing to living abundantly, you will know the fullness of joy, and your plate will be heaped with good things.

> May you experience the love of Christ, though it is too great to understand fully. Then you will be made complete with all the fullness of life and power that comes from God.

> —Ephesians 3:19 NLT

MY SNUGGLER

And I will pray the Father, and he shall give you another
Comforter, that he may be with you forever...

—John 14:16 ASV

My son has never been a good sleeper. I (vaguely) remember the first
three months of his life, desperately trying to get his sleep schedule
right side up. He slept during the day, woke up with a vengeance at
dinnertime, went down around 8:00 p.m., and woke back up at precisely
eleven o'clock. He would fall back to sleep at 1:00 a.m., only to wake up
again two hours later. He'd go back to sleep at 5:00 a.m.

Then Caitlyn would wake up at six.

It was rough.

At twenty months, he gave us our very first night of (almost)
uninterrupted sleep. While those days are behind us, the memory is
vivid enough to cap our childbearing at two.

Nick no longer cries out in the middle of the night when he wakes
up. Instead, he rolls out of bed and makes his way into our room. Mike,
being a lighter sleeper, can usually be counted on to promptly carry
him back. Nick, figuring this out, has come up with a solution: stay on
mom's side of the bed.

It is not uncommon for me to wake up in the wee hours of the night
with my little boy burrowing into my side. In fact, every once in a while,
I wake up with my son, quite literally, sprawled out *on me*.

"Why don't you just move him back?" my husband asked
incredulously as I complained about (another) poor night's sleep.

"I know," I sighed. "Two reasons. I'm too tired to move, and I love how he snuggles into me. These days will be over in a heartbeat and then I'll miss them."

Mike shook his head and shrugged his shoulders. I guess it's a mom thing.

> When doubts filled my mind, your comfort gave me
> renewed hope and cheer.
>
> —Psalm 94:19 NLT

Of all the magnificent and majestic names the Holy Spirit assumes, Comforter is the one I love most. God is the Rock and our refuge, an ever-present help in trouble; He is our rescuer and the Redeemer, a mighty fortress for all who seek shelter in Him. He is the wonderful Counselor, the Alpha and Omega, the Prince of Peace, and our everlasting Father.

He is also our Comforter. And we are a people in desperate need of comfort.

> These things have I spoken unto you, while yet abiding with you. But the Comforter, even the Holy Spirit, whom the Father will send in my name, he shall teach you all things, and bring to your remembrance all that I said unto you.
>
> —John 14:25–26 ASV

The night before Christ went to the cross, His primary concern was comforting and reassuring the disciples. Two-thousand years later, His heart has not changed. He longs to comfort you.

When Nick wakes up in the middle of the night, he needs the reassurance of my presence. Being near me isn't enough. He burrows into my side, getting as close as he possibly can, then closer still.

Oh, that we would do the same.

What is troubling you? Burrow into the comfort of Christ. Let's go beyond merely visiting Him for an hour or so on Sunday. Let's seek His face in all that we do. Let's invite the Holy Spirit into our hearts, allowing Him full access to every area of our lives. Instead of exhausting ourselves on the treadmill of self-sustained effort, let's walk in daily surrender, remembering that He who gave His only Son for us will never forsake us.

That is where our comfort lies. Not in more things or fewer pounds. Not in money, power, or accolades. Our comfort and consolation comes from pressing into the heart of Christ and allowing the Holy Spirit to transform us from the inside out.

> I am leaving you with a gift—peace of mind and heart.
> And the peace I give isn't like the peace the world gives.
> So don't be troubled or afraid.
>
> —John 14:27 NLT

MOMMY LOVE

Long ago the Lord said to Israel: "I have loved you, my people, with an everlasting love. With unfailing love I have drawn you to myself."

—Jeremiah, 31:3 NLT

Crash!
   Bang!
   "Mommy!"
   As a mother of young children, the preceding scenario is a familiar one. It seems as though at least once a day, one of my children is falling off a couch, a bike, a scooter, or any number of things that cause both a fright and an attention-demanding boo-boo.
   How I love this stage, where only a mommy's kiss can fix it.
   The trauma is not always physical. Not long ago, my son raced toward me, sobbing uncontrollably and tears streaming down his face. My daughter and our neighbor's two children didn't want to play the game that Nick did, and the playdate quickly unraveled.
   I scooped my son up in my arms and held him close.
   "Oh, honey, I love you so much. Mommy loves you so much. Shh."
   After a few minutes, my son calmed down enough to talk about it, and we found a solution.
   Later in the day, my daughter and I were riding bikes when a sharp turn and a pile of sand got the best of her and down she went. I raced to her side, gathered her in my arms, and calmed her down in the same way.
   "I know, honey. I know. Come here. Mommy loves you so much."

Moments later, we were on our way.

Isn't it interesting that no matter the occasion for tears, my immediate reaction is always the same? I gather them in my arms. I hold them as tightly as I can, and I tell them over and over that I love them. It is not a planned response. I don't think it through. My instinct is to reassure them with my love, and no matter the problem, it is my love for them that calms them down.

> I have loved you even as the Father has loved me. Remain in my love.
>
> —John 15:9 NLT

The night before He went to the cross, Jesus spent His remaining time illustrating His love for His disciples. His predominant concern was their peace of mind. He warned them of trials, difficulties, and persecution. His solution was always the same: "Remain in my love."

I can't fix the majority of the problems my children will face. I have no intention of pretending that I can. Even if I could, I wouldn't.

They need to learn how to resolve conflict in a mature and respectful way. They must go through adversity to gain moral character and endure pain to grow in compassion and empathy. They'll learn patience through persevering and endurance through suffering.

I love them too much to rob them of that. But my promise to them, now and always, is to love them through everything.

I will walk with them through the deepest valleys. I will stay by their side through the darkest nights. Their mistakes will never outweigh my love. They cannot stray so far from the path that I cannot not find them. There is no price too great to buy them back from the farthest reaches of sin, even if it means my life.

That's how Jesus loves you. He loved you before the world began. He loved you as He hung on the cross. His love is wrapped around you, and it will carry you over the threshold as you pass from this life to the next.

May the comfort of the Comforter reassure you now and always as you remain in His love.

I pray for them. I am not praying for the world but for those You have given Me, because they are Yours. Everything I have is Yours, and everything You have is Mine, and I have been glorified in them. I am no longer in the world, but they are in the world, and I am coming to You. Holy Father, protect them by Your name that You have given Me, so that they may be one as We are one.

—John 17:9–11 HCSB

HIGH SCHOOL TRACK

These trials will show that your faith is genuine. It is
being tested as fire tests and purifies gold—though your
faith is far more precious than mere gold. So when your
faith remains strong through many trials, it will bring
you much praise and glory and honor on the day when
Jesus Christ is revealed to the whole world.

—1 Peter 1:7 NLT

I owe my love of running to my dad.

My dad is an accomplished marathoner, boasting ten completed 26.3
mile races. Of course, he's now boasting two shiny new hips because of
it, but that's another story for another time.

As a little girl, my parents would drive my sisters and me to the
high school track and "let" us run if we were well-behaved (brilliant
parenting, by the way). My sisters carried on the family tradition, joining
track as soon as they could, but I allowed my love of theater to override
my Nikes and fell away during my tween and early teen years.

Fast forward to 1992.

As a senior in high school, I was overweight, suffering from low
(read "no") self-esteem, flirting with an eating disorder, and miserable.
My father, tired of the complaining, threw down a mandate: run track
or be grounded for the rest of your senior year (a missing tidbit of info
is that this mandate came on the heels of getting caught, overserved, on
school grounds). I chose track.

It was a decision that changed the course of my life.

I filed onto the track with the rest of the team on the first day. The cool mountain breeze cut easily through my thin T-shirt, and I shivered. My mind grasped for an excuse not to run. Finding none, I sighed and turned my attention to the coach.

Standing at 5 feet, 8 inches tall, Gary Liese was sturdy and built—an accomplished sprinter in his day. His eyes danced merrily as a mischievous grin pulled at the corner of his lips. He fingered the shiny whistle hanging around his neck, put it to his lips, and blew.

"Alright, everyone," he cried. "Let's see what you've got! Timed miles. Let's go, let's go, let's go!"

A timed mile is four laps around the track, running as fast as you could go. The good runners finished it in six minutes. The great runners came in at five-and-a-half. I clocked in at a shade over eight and thought I was dying.

Coach Liese never went easy on me, even though there were many other runners far more worthy of his attention and efforts. As we moved into the fourth and final quarter of the year, he encouraged me to sign up for his strength and conditioning class, promising that the workouts would improve my running.

Why does he care? I wondered. *I'm getting ready to graduate.* Reluctantly, under his less-than-gentle prodding, I took the class.

I came to respect the executor of my torture, realizing that the old me had to be broken down if the new me were to emerge.

I started to push myself harder. If he said, "Run five miles this weekend," I ran seven. I altered my diet and streamlined my lifestyle, and at the regional track meet—the state meet qualifier—I saw the fruit of my efforts.

I shaved over two-and-a-half minutes off my mile and ran the fastest two-mile race of my life.

It took every ounce of strength I had. I did not qualify for the state meet, but I accomplished far more than I'd ever dreamed possible all because of a coach who would not give up on an overweight, insecure, rookie senior.

Dear brothers and sisters, when troubles come your way, consider it an opportunity for great joy. For you know

that when your faith is tested, your endurance has a
chance to grow. So let it grow, for when your endurance
is fully developed, you will be perfect and complete,
needing nothing.

—James 1:2–4 NLT

At the team banquet, I watched as the staff passed out awards. I
beamed, heart bursting, as my sister and her relay team raised their
trophies. I knew that my name would not be called, but I had never felt
so full. It was the first time I had truly pushed myself out of my comfort
zone to accomplish a goal.

"And most improved goes to…Rebecca Ashbrook!"

A lump formed in my throat as I weaved my way to the front of the
room. Beaming, Coach Liese handed me the medal and pulled me in
for a hug. "I never let up on you, kiddo," he whispered, "because I knew
you had it in you. I knew it!"

What a beautiful thing to know that someone sees *more* when they
look at you.

May you experience the love of Christ, though it is
too great to understand fully. Then you will be made
complete with all the fullness of life and power that
comes from God.

—Ephesians 3:19 NLT

What do you see when you look in the mirror?

Friend, God sees *more.* And just as my track coach pushed me and
worked me until I could barely stand it, God will work you and push you
until you fulfill the glorious purpose He has called you to. He will make
things uncomfortable. He will cut away relationships. He will chip away
at your pride and sand down your rough edges. He will put people in
your path to irritate you, exposing character traits within you that need
to go, so you can become a reflection of Jesus.

He loves you too much not to. He sees too much potential in you to
let you stay the way you are.

Why do we go through adversity? Instead of answering that question, I will leave you with something that God pressed on me:

A life without adversity is a life lacking true strength, earned wisdom, and an empathetic heart.

God bless you.

THE APARTMENT

For our present troubles are small and won't last
very long. Yet they produce for us a glory that vastly
outweighs them and will last forever!

—2 Corinthians 4:17 NLT

I am so jealous.

Not the mean-spirited-wish-bad-things-on-someone kind of
jealousy, but rather the wistful-wishful-slightly-sad kind.

My two younger sisters live in the Kansas City area. They are both
married with three kids.

And they live across the street from each other.

Yes, across the street.

I love visiting. There is no "whose house should we stay at" decision
to make because when you live across the street from each other, it
doesn't matter.

Instead of two families, my sisters, their husbands, and children are
one big happy family. They eat dinner at each other's houses, watch each
other's kids, and do life together.

Here is how it happened. My youngest sister, Emily, bought a house
in a cute little cul-de-sac. Shortly after, the house across the street hit
the market.

There was one small problem—it was a tiny, two-bedroom house,
and my middle sister, Liz, needed something bigger for her family of
five (seven if you count the two golden retrievers).

The solution? Build up.

So that's what they did. They hired a contractor and moved out of their house and into a nine-hundred-square-foot apartment.

Eager to see my sisters and their new homes, the kids and I drove up.

> So we don't look at the troubles we can see now; rather, we fix our gaze on things that cannot be seen. For the things we see now will soon be gone, but the things we cannot see will last forever.
>
> —2 Corinthians 4:18 NLT

Liz warned me that it was cramped.

"And I haven't done a thing to it," she added, leading the kids and I through the front door.

She was right. Stark white walls boasted no room-warming pictures and only the bare essentials for furniture. There were no curtains on the windows and no rugs on the floors. It was clear this was not where Liz was focusing her attention.

"I bet you're ready to get out of here," I said to Liz, smiling.

"Oh, you know, it's not too bad," she replied. "I've been so busy working on the new house that I don't even really see it."

I nodded in agreement. I know what it's like to be so wrapped up in something that your current circumstances fade into the background. Plus, there's no sense putting much time and energy into the temporary when you could invest in the permanent.

If only we could wrap our hearts and minds around that once and for all.

> Don't store up treasures here on earth, where moths eat them and rust destroys them, and where thieves break in and steal. Store your treasures in heaven, where moths and rust cannot destroy, and thieves do not break in and steal. Wherever your treasure is, there the desires of your heart will also be.
>
> —Matthew 6:19–21 NLT

The New Testament was originally written in Greek, and the word translated to *heart* is καρδία (kardia). It means "the seat of thought and emotion." Jesus is encouraging us to fix our thoughts on heaven.

Imagine the peace and freedom we'd enjoy if we would remember that our current circumstances are temporary housing when compared with eternity.

What are you worried about? No matter how big it looks right now, it is temporary. What keeps you awake at night? God is aware of it. What is stealing your attention away from heavenly things? Your heavenly Father is jealous for your every thought. He gave you this life; He wants you to enjoy it and to know the richness and abundance you have in Christ.

But He also wants you to know this: compared to the glory awaiting you, this life is a nine-hundred-square- foot apartment.

Don't be so concerned with what goes on the walls. Don't worry too much about rugs on the floors. Don't be preoccupied with gadgets, knickknacks, and stuff. Instead, let your mind wander to the things of Christ.

Dwell on His Word. Linger in His Presence. Breathe in His Spirit. Live out His love.

> Therefore if you have been raised up with Christ, keep seeking the things above, where Christ is, seated at the right hand of God. Set your mind on the things above, not on the things that are on earth. For you have died and your life is hidden with Christ in God. When Christ, who is our life, is revealed, then you also will be revealed with Him in glory.
>
> —Colossians 3:1–4 NASB

THE BATHROOM WALL

For I am confident of this very thing, that He who began
a good work in you will perfect it until the day of Christ
Jesus.

—Philippians1:6 NASB

My husband will never, ever let me attempt another home improvement
project ever again.

We moved into our current home in September of 2008. In October,
I decided to paint our downstairs bathroom. I chose the color and bought
the paint. I taped the floor and ceiling and set to work.

I almost finished it.

In November of the same year, I told my husband that I wanted to
completely redo our children's Jack & Jill bathroom. I wrenched the
towel racks off of the walls in anticipation of the brushed nickel ones I
wanted to buy.

That's as far as I got.

I have good intentions, I really do, but sometimes I get distracted.

My dresser is stacked with half-finished books. My computer is
filled with half-completed articles. Our laundry room has baskets of
half-folded clothes and, as I type, our sink is half-full of dishes.

I am so glad God is not like me.

The Lord will accomplish what concerns me;
Your loving kindness, O Lord, is everlasting; Do not
forsake the works of Your hands.

—Psalm 138:8 NASB

God does not suffer from attention deficit disorder. He does not get distracted by a prayer request. He doesn't lose interest in things halfway through. He doesn't start a project enthusiastically, then change His mind when things go south.

Today, meditate on this: God sees something precious and priceless in you. While we get caught up in our flaws and failures, God sees past that to our *potential.* When a sculptor looks at a block of lumber, he sees past the wood—he sees the masterpiece.

You, friend, are God's masterpiece. He keeps you close to His to heart and gently, over time, prunes away the unfruitful branches and sands down the rough edges. Like a skillful potter with a lump of clay, He applies pressure when necessary, all the while holding you in His hands.

He has a plan for you. You are where you are by divine design. He will never give up on you and will never fail you or forsake you. He promises you this: when He is finished with you, you will be *glorious.*

The nations will see your righteousness. World leaders
will be blinded by your glory. And you will be given a
new name by the Lord's own mouth. The Lord will hold
you in his hand for all to see— a splendid crown in the
hand of God.

—Isaiah 62:2–3 NLT

MOUNTAIN DEW, HEADACHES, AND GRACE

As you know, like a father with his own children, we encouraged, comforted, and implored each one of you to walk worthy of God, who calls you into His own kingdom and glory.

—1 Thessalonians 2:11–12 HCSB

I get a wee bit frustrated (in a nurturing, sisterly way) with my morning show cohost on 90.9 KCBI. His name is Jeff Taylor.

Jeff subsists on a diet of Mountain Dew, Twinkies, and steak.

Oh wait, he likes coffee too.

Jeff Taylor also gets kidney stones.

You know what is not good for kidney stones? Mountain Dew and coffee.

You know what *is* helpful with kidney stones? Lots of water.

Guess what Jeff won't drink?

Sigh.

I have a friend who gets terrible headaches.

"Why don't you take something?" I ask.

"No, I don't need anything."

Sigh.

This is kind of like me with grace.

Don't get me wrong—I *love* grace. I'm desperate for grace. I need grace like I need air—every minute of every day.

So why do I resist it so much? Why do I try so hard to prove myself, as though I could win points with God? Why do I act like Jeff with his kidney stones or my friend and her headaches? I push, pull, and strain against the very thing—the *only* thing—that brings relief.

I know these things, but I still find myself living a life contrary to grace. Pastor and author Tullian Tchividjian calls it the trap of "do-more-try-harder."

I'm not alone, am I? Do we not all operate, at some level, under the guise that if we do more and try harder, we will somehow increase our worth? We wear busyness like a badge of honor, as though the more harried we become, the godlier we appear.

This notion was driven home for me recently by an e-mail from a dear friend. This is a small portion of it:

> I miss our talks too. I tell you, Rebecca, over the last couple of months, I have been hurt so badly by people I love so dearly. I am realizing how much I need the Lord. I have realized how many things I did to get approval from people. I have stopped. I have been praying and thinking hard on every action I take. Is it for the glory of God, to please people, or to try to be good enough? I'm realizing a lot about myself. It is a good time, but heartbreaking all the same. I love you and hope to get to spend some quality time with you soon.

It was like reading a page from my journal.

This is the response I sent. Little does she know that I needed to read it more than she did. Maybe you do too.

> Hey, sweet friend. I know just how you feel. Been there, been there, been there!
>
> I am sorry you've been hurt. I hope I am not one of the people who have hurt you! And please don't feel down about yourself and the things that the Lord is revealing to you. I know you know this, but He convicts because He loves. And if we are constantly being made over into the image of Christ, that means we are constantly being poked, prodded, squeezed, pressed,

and shaken. It won't end until we graduate from skin to glory.

Here is what you need to swim around in for a while: because of the cross, there is nothing, *not one thing*, you can do to make yourself more acceptable to Him. Because of Jesus, His delight in you will never run dry—not even on your worst day. He is not now nor will He ever be angry at you because He exhausted His anger on Christ. And as hard as you try to be holy, you will still struggle with pride. You will still judge people. You will say things you shouldn't say and think things you shouldn't think. His grace has already covered those sins. The only thing you and I bring to our salvation is the sin that makes it necessary (thank you, Pastor Tchividjian).

Think about this: as much as a six-year-old wants to ride a bike on the first try, it takes time, practice, and bruised knees. Doing things well requires perseverance and patience. As much as you and I want to be sanctified now, it takes a lifetime of walking with the Lord.

So just *breathe*.

He loves you. It's not about how well you love Him. You don't love Him with your whole heart, mind, soul, and strength—you can't. But that's okay because it's not about you loving Him. It's about Him loving you.

It's not about you holding onto Him. It's about Him never letting go of you.

It's not about your sinlessness or you sinning less. It's about Him fulfilling the law perfectly and absorbing the wrath of a holy God. Why? Because we are sinners, and He is stronger than our sin.

It's not even about your faithfulness. You only have faith because He planted it in you. It is about His faithfulness no matter how many times you fail Him. You will fail Him again, and He knows it. Yet He still chose the cross.

That's what grace is.
Grace is pretty cool, huh?
I love you, friend. Let's go walking soon.

Much love,
Rebecca

The Word became flesh and took up residence among us. We observed His glory, the glory as the One and Only Son from the Father, full of grace and truth.

—John 1:14 HCSB

STINKY GYM CLOTHES

I will rejoice greatly in the Lord, my soul will exult in my
God; for He has clothed me with garments of salvation,
He has wrapped me with a robe of righteousness, as a
bridegroom decks himself with a garland, and as a bride
adorns herself with her jewels.

—Isaiah 61:10 NASB

Gym showers creep some people out.

Not me.

I like to shower at the gym for two reasons: First, it's the only time I
get to take a shower without fear of children barging in on me. Second,
the water pressure is wonderful. Feeling earthy, my husband and I put
water-saver shower heads in our bathrooms. They're good in theory,
but not so good when I'm in a hurry and need to get the conditioner out
of my hair.

One time, after an especially brutal workout, I stood under that
blessed water pressure for at least ten minutes while the heat soothed
my worn-out muscles.

Covered in two towels (uber modest), I made my way to my locker.
I turned the lock and opened the door to see an empty gym bag.

I'd forgotten a change of clothes.

In disbelief, I looked at my sweaty, stinky pile of workout clothes.

Quickly, my mind flipped through a list of alternatives. I couldn't
call my husband to bring an outfit because he was at work forty-five
minutes away. A friend? Not enough time. I had only 20 more minutes

before my two-hour limit was up in the childcare center. Steal the towels and duck out the back?

With grim resolution, I picked up the clothes and carried them, at arm's length, to a changing stall. Then I put the sweaty, yucky, damp, stinky clothes on my fresh, clean skin.

Nothing, and I mean not one thing, feels worse on clean skin than sweaty, yucky, damp, stinky gym clothes.

> But let us who live in the light be clearheaded, protected by the armor of faith and love, and wearing as our helmet the confidence of our salvation. For God chose to save us through our Lord Jesus Christ, not to pour out his anger on us.
>
> —1 Thessalonians 5:8–9 NLT

If we are believers in Christ, we are saved. If we are saved, we are clean. And if we are clean, let us clothe ourselves in fresh garments.

Sometimes I find myself slipping back into my spiritual stinky gym gear...

...when I selfishly try to manipulate and maneuver circumstances to go my way.

...when the need to be right overrides the desire to be kind.

...when I take advantage of my husband's grace and let the laundry pile grow and grow.

...when I park the kids in front of the TV instead of taking them to a park.

...when I slip into work fifteen minutes later than I should.

...when I sit by in silence instead of speaking up.

...when I say stupid things to win approval.

...when I chase after anything other than God.

Over and over again in Scripture, God offers us a "robe of righteousness." Righteousness is not something we can conjure up within ourselves; therefore, God has to cloak us in it. We can't be righteous in our own strength; therefore we must wear the righteousness of Christ.

We have to purposefully and intentionally take off that which comes naturally for us and put on the attributes of Jesus.

When I find myself getting angry at inconsequential things, I say, "Stinky gym clothes!" The old Rebecca would put on anger. I don't have to wear that anymore, so I ask God to cover me with a mantle of patience.

When I find myself worrying about whether or not so-and-so likes me or what someone else thinks of me, I picture myself throwing my stinky gym clothes into the washing machine.

I can choose to wear something else. I can choose to dwell on the fact that God is pleased with me because I am in Christ.

He is pleased with you too—Not because of anything you do, but because of what Jesus did. Not because of your faithfulness, but because of Jesus' faithfulness. Not because of who you are, but because of who you are in Christ.

In Christ, you are adopted, adored, and adorned in a robe of righteousness.

You are clean.

> Let us rejoice and be glad and give the glory to Him,
> for the marriage of the Lamb has come and His bride
> has made herself ready." It was given to her to clothe
> herself in fine linen, bright and clean; for the fine linen
> is the righteous acts of the saints.
>
> —Revelation 19:7–8 NASB

A CHRISTMAS MIRACLE

> I want you to show love, not offer sacrifices. I want you
> to know me more than I want burnt offerings.
>
> —Hosea 6:6 NLT

I will never forget the Christmas of 2011. That was the year of the Christmas miracle.

I almost missed it.

My Sunday school class had adopted a family from Sunlight Missionary Baptist Church in south Dallas. Sunlight is a small building complete with bars on the windows and doors. Visit on a summer day, and you'll notice the absence of an air conditioner. Drop by in the winter, and you'll see congregants wrapped in their coats, if they have one. Regardless of the weather, folks faithfully gather every Sunday to hear the hope and encouragement of Christ given by Pastor Ed.

As a Christmas mission, my class collected money and various items in order to give needy families bags full of gifts and necessities. The following Saturday, several of them (not me) caravanned south to deliver the goodies.

But one little boy was left out. Somehow, his name had been left off the list, and he got nothing—no clothes and no toys.

Moved with compassion, one woman (not me) led the charge to put together a goody bag for the devastated child.

A few days later, I, along with my children and two members of the class (we'll call them Mike and Kathy), delivered the gifts.

I almost didn't go.

When God's people are in need, be ready to help them.
Always be eager to practice hospitality.

—Romans 12:13 NLT

An e-mail went out a few days prior to delivery day (d-day) calling all-hands-on-deck to make the trip. Although I work mornings, I was available to go. I knew I *should* go. I knew it would bless my kids.

I just didn't *want* to go.

I waited a few hours, ignoring my nagging conscience. Then I sent the following response: "What time are you leaving?" Mike responded quickly, letting me know that others had signed on, and while I was more than welcome to help, there was no longer a sense of urgency.

The next morning, I opened my inbox to the following email from another member of the class: "Rebecca, if you can go, it would be an incredible blessing for you and your kids." The note was signed "Rob," but I knew better. It was a direct word from God.

By evening, I still hadn't responded, and the nudge from the Holy Spirit was growing in strength and intensity. Early on d-day, I sent another e-mail: "Hi, Mike, do you have it covered?"

It's probably too late by now, I thought to myself. A minute later, my phone chirped cheerfully, indicating a new message in my inbox.

"Not too late, and we could certainly use the help," Mike wrote. At this point, I started to connive. After all, I really wanted to go to the gym, and this would be my last chance before the holiday feasting ensued.

As I began to plot and plan, formulating excuses in my mind, the Holy Spirit interrupted me with two simple words: "Choose *me*."

I sighed, shaking my head. God was putting this family on my heart. He showed me that, by obeying, He would not only bless and minister to this family, He would bless me and my children too.

Okay, Lord, I silently prayed. *And please forgive my selfishness.*

You can make this choice by loving the Lord your God,
obeying him, and committing yourself firmly to him.
This is the key to your life. And if you love and obey

the Lord, you will live long in the land the Lord swore
to give your ancestors Abraham, Isaac, and Jacob.

—Deuteronomy 30:20 NLT

Loaded with packages, we pulled into the apartment complex. My
children and I were among the first to enter, and what I saw broke my
heart.

The apartment couldn't have been more than seven or eight hundred
square feet, and it housed four children and five adults. There were no
beds and no furniture, except for two small couches that scarcely fit
in the living room. Lying on one couch was a small woman who'd had
both legs amputated.

We filled that room with presents, supplies, and a Christmas
tree. When we were finished, I walked over to the bedridden woman
and knelt by her side. We chatted for a few minutes, then we prayed.
I held her hands and kissed her cheek. When I asked her how I could
continue to pray for her, she started to cry. Barely able to get the words
out, she whispered that she needed a wheelchair so that she could go to
church more often. The one she had didn't work, and she wanted to go
to the Christmas service.

"Comfort, comfort my people," says your God.

—Isaiah 40:1 NLT

All week long at 90.9 KCBI, we'd been asking listeners to call and
share their Christmas miracles. And save one or two stories, *all* of the
miracles had been through acts of human kindness and generosity. "You
be the miracle," whispered the Spirit. *"You be My hands and feet."*

The next morning, I shared the experience on the air. The listeners'
response brought me to tears. A generous dentist in the area called in
wanting to help. A woman offered one-hundred dollars. Call after call
came until a man named Bruce offered up a wheelchair that belonged
to a friend who had recently passed.

"I've tried to sell it on Craigslist and eBay," he said. "Now I know
why it didn't sell."

Today I have given you the choice between life and death, between blessings and curses. Now I call on heaven and earth to witness the choice you make. Oh, that you would choose life, so that you and your descendants might live!

—Deuteronomy 30:19 NLT

I almost chose the gym. I went to Sunlight begrudgingly, even sullenly, more out of guilt than love. As I think of the way God has blessed my family and compare it to that precious family's conditions, I get teary again. God forgave my selfishness, but I can't forget how close I came to missing a chain reaction of blessings.

Had I ignored the nudge of the Holy Spirit, I would've missed the look on the faces of the children as they opened their gifts, not to mention the look on the faces of my four- and five-year-olds as they watched. I would've missed the forty-five-minute-long conversation we had driving home on the true meaning of Christmas. I would've lost the opportunity to meet Pastor Ed. I would've missed the tremendous honor of praying with and over the sweet lady on the couch, and I would not have learned of her need.

Had I chosen the gym, I would've robbed many listeners of the chance to bless another family in need, and I would've denied Bruce the awesome display of God's hand at work in something as small as a wheelchair he couldn't sell.

There is nothing special or remarkable about me. God doesn't speak to me any more frequently than He speaks to you. But in order to hear His voice, we *must* remain tuned in to the Holy Spirit. 1 Thessalonians 5:19 says, "Do not stifle the Holy Spirit" (NLT). We stifle the Spirit when we ignore nudges and whispers. The more we stifle them, the fainter they become.

Is the Holy Spirit nudging you through my confession? Pay attention. Jesus has no physical body on this earth. Therefore, we must lend Him ours. Sometimes we're asked to pray for a miracle. More often, we're called to *be* one.

IDENTITY CRISIS

See how great a love the Father has bestowed on us, that
we would be called children of God; and such we are.
For this reason the world does not know us, because it
did not know Him.

—1 John 3:1 NASB

"So, what do you do?"

The question always comes up. And it always makes me squirm.

My typical answer is three-fold: "Well, I'm a wife and mother first. I
have a Women's Ministry called 'LSS Ministries,' and I also work at a
radio station."

I get that glazed-over-pretending-to-be-interested look until I hit
answer number three. Then eyebrows shoot up, and all of the sudden, I
rank as a person worthy of conversing with. I understand it's an unusual
career and one people might be curious about. But it saddens me a wee
bit when I perceive that the only reason someone is interested in me is
because of my job.

I'm more than my job. Aren't you?

Let's talk about jobs for a moment.

The radio industry is a casualty of the economy or, perhaps, of
technology. Either way, I've had a lot of conversations with fallen
comrades over the past few years. They are amazing, talented individuals
who were once making a nice living in an industry chock full of perks.
They are now limping along, wondering what in the world they'll do
now that their field of expertise has dwindled to a shadow of what it
once was.

The lesson I've learned watching the career slaughter is this: when we let what we do define who we are, we will fall victim to life's inevitable circumstances.

By the nature of my job, I meet people of notoriety every now and then. I've generalized them into two categories:

Category one: The Self-Consumed. When you ask SCs how they are, the conversation revolves around their accomplishments and things they're working on. A typical answer is, "Man, just lovin' life on the road, you know? There's just nothing better than walking out on that stage, hearing the roar of the crowd, listening them sing your songs word for word. Got the new album coming out...and we think that's really gonna take things to the next level."

Category two: The Terry Bradshaws. One morning, during my time at 96.3 KSCS, Terry Bradshaw came in to hang out on the show. He talked about his Bible study and his family. He preferred asking questions to answering them. We could scarcely get him to talk about himself because he simply wasn't self-absorbed. He was more interested in others.

At the end of the day, which category will be more likely to roll with life's punches when life punches them in the nose?

Earlier in my career, I worked the night show at another station. My hours were 7:00 p.m. to 11:00 p.m. I had the entire day to devote myself to other things. No husband, no kids—just hours and hours of availability.

Here is how I spent my time: I got up around 9:45 a.m., watched *The View*, ate breakfast, hit the gym, made lunch, read by the pool (weather permitting), thought about how depressed I was, and went to work.

I was miserable.

I had no purpose aside from my four-hour-a-day job.

Imagine if I'd lost it. My purpose, my identity, and my self-esteem would've shattered.

God created us *on* purpose, *with* purpose, to live *purposefully*. But God doesn't define us by what we do. Over and over again in Scripture, he defines us as His children, made in His image, made righteous by the blood of His Son, not the sweat of our brow.

Let your roots grow down into him, and let your lives be built on him. Then your faith will grow strong in the truth you were taught, and you will overflow with thankfulness.

—Colossians 2:7 NLT

What are you rooted in? Children grow up, marriages dissolve, people pass away, jobs vanish, and beauty fades. In the gospel of Luke, Jesus says, "Heaven and earth will disappear, but my words will remain forever (Luke 21:33 NLT)."

Friend, you are His. Let that be forever enough.

THE CHALLENGE FLAG

I—yes, I alone—will blot out your sins for my own sake and will never think of them again. Let us review the situation together, and you can present your case to prove your innocence.

—Isaiah 43:25–26 NLT

Aside from God and family, my husband lives for one thing: football season.

From February to August, Mike tracks scouting and recruiting. He eagerly anticipates training camp, and he counts down the days to the preseason. While everyone else watches dismissively, Mike is eyeing and evaluating new players and play calling. And the first home game of the year? You would think it was a national holiday.

To avoid a widow-like state during these months, I have allowed my husband to educate me on the finer points of football, and surprised myself by becoming a bona fide fan.

A fun bonus? The theology I've discovered along the way. Football provides some marvelous biblical analogies.

Consider the challenge flag.

If the coach disagrees with a referee's ruling on the field, he can throw the challenge flag. Enter the instant replay. The referees will review the footage from every camera angle, and we follow along at home. If the officials agree with the coach, they reverse their call. If they disagree, the challenging team is penalized with a time-out.

One day the members of the heavenly court came to present themselves before the Lord, and the Accuser, Satan, came with them.

"Where have you come from?" the Lord asked Satan. Satan answered the Lord, "I have been patrolling the earth, watching everything that's going on."

—Job 1:6–7 NLT

Throughout the Bible, Satan has many names. "The Accuser" resonates deeply with me. He and I have a history. Throughout the years, he has told me things like:

"Why did you eat that? You have no self-control!"
"You're an idiot. You're ugly. No one will ever love you."
"You don't have the education to teach or speak. Who do you think you are? You'll never be anything for God."
"You'll never be as good as she is. Just quit."
"How could you do that? How could you say something like that?"

The Accuser loves to point out our fouls, falls, and fails. He replays them in slow motion, from every vantage point, over and over and over again.

On this side of heaven, we will always struggle with sin. We do the wrong thing for no reason and the right thing with the wrong motives. King David found comfort in the Lord: "You know what I am going to say even before I say it, Lord" (Psalm 139:4 NLT).

God knew the mistakes you would make before you made them, and He still saved you. God knows where and when we will fall short, and He still chose the cross. Because Jesus paid the penalty, every moment is another chance to wipe our slate, and the scoreboard, clean.

We are made right with God by placing our faith in Jesus Christ. And this is true for everyone who believes, no matter who we are. For everyone has sinned; we

all fall short of God's glorious standard. Yet God, with
undeserved kindness, declares that we are righteous. He
did this through Christ Jesus when he freed us from the
penalty for our sins.

—Romans 3:22–24 NLT

Did you catch that? "He freed us from the penalty for our sins."

That means you are free to run, play, try, fall, and get back up and
try again.

When Satan throws the challenge flag, remember that you have a
choice. You don't have to review the footage.

You don't have to relive your sins and mistakes. The enemy would
have you replay the incident over and over in your mind, analyzing it
from every angle, filling your head with self-defeating commentary. But
here is something straight from our holy playbook: you have the power
to choose your thoughts.

We demolish arguments and every pretension that sets
itself up against the knowledge of God, and we take
captive every thought to make it obedient to Christ.

—2 Corinthians 10:5 NIV

And how do we do this? With the same divine power God used to
raise Christ from the grave.

We use God's mighty weapons, not worldly weapons, to
knock down the strongholds of human reasoning and to
destroy false arguments.

—2 Corinthians 10:4 NLT

The next time the Accuser throws the challenge flag on your past, hear the words of the great Referee: "The ruling on the field stands. The challenging team with be charged with one time-out."

> "Even from eternity I am He, and there is none who can deliver out of My hand; I act and who can reverse it?"

—Isaiah 43:13 NASB

FINAL THOUGHTS

Not long ago I was asked to give a devotion to the staff of the Dallas branch of *Apartment Life*[7] – a ministry that places team members in apartment complexes to open up opportunities to share the gospel.

Mike Tirone, the President, invited me to share "whatever God has lain on your heart."

That's like sending a kid into the world's biggest candy store with two dollars and saying, "Pick out one thing!"

So many verses, so many topics, so many things I could talk about – what would I choose?

I began to journal, asking the Lord to direct my thoughts and my study. As I wrote, the only thing I could think about was how much I love His Word.

The most precious times in my life have been spent in solitude, with a candle lit, a cup of coffee, and a pen. With my journal and Bible open, Jesus and I have walked through the Garden of Eden in the cool of the day, we've watched breathlessly as David toppled the giant, and we've wept at the gravesite of Lazarus.

I would not trade a single moment in His Presence for all the money, fame, or accolades in the world.

So that was it. That was what I would share with the group – *Falling in love with God through His Word*. Would you allow me to share it with you?

First, a note about His Word. When you study the Bible, study it with the purpose of discovering who God is. Don't play *Bible Roulette* by asking God a question, flipping through the pages, and randomly landing on a verse.

---

[7]   Apartment Life. http://www.apartmentlife.org/Home/tabid/651/Default.aspx

Keep in mind that the Bible is not an à la carte café. Paul wrote Timothy to encourage him in his study, reminding him that "all Scripture is inspired by God and is useful to teach us what is true and to make us realize what is wrong in our lives. It corrects us when we are wrong and teaches us to do what is right."[8] Move out of your comfort zone by reading the books you don't understand. Ask yourself as you read how they fit into the grand plan of redemption.

In her book, *Women of the Word: How to Study the Bible with Both Our Hearts and Our Minds,* Jen Wilkin reminds us that the Bible is a book about God, not a book about us. In *The Epic of Eden: A Christian Entry into the Old Testament,* Sandra L. Richter describes the Bible's objective—"to tell the epic tale of God's ongoing quest to ransom His creation"[9] through the sacrifice of His only Son.

Read the Bible one book at a time. Before you start reading the text, research the book for a few minutes. Who wrote it? When was it written? To whom was it written? How does it fit into the story of creation, fall, and redemption?

Then read the book slowly. Pray as you go. Jot down any questions you have, and highlight passages that speak to you. Why do they speak to you? Journaling through the Bible has been like an ongoing treasure hunt—never failing to surprise and delight me.

At present, I am studying the book of John. Again. And as is so often the case, a phrase popped out at me that I had never noticed before.

> While He was in Jerusalem at the Passover Festival, many trusted in His name when they saw the signs He was doing. Jesus, however, would not entrust Himself to them, since He knew them all and because He did not need anyone to testify about man; for He Himself knew what was in man.

> —John 2:23-25 HCSB

---

8   2 Timothy 3:16 NLT

9   Sandra L. Richter, *The Epic of Eden: A Christian Entry into the Old Testament* (InterVarsity Press, 2008), p. 15

What a provocative notion – the people saw and believed, they trusted in His name, but Jesus would not entrust Himself to them. Why? Because they were not coming to Him for *Him*. They were coming to Him for what He could *do* for them.

And therein lies the answer to our every question, ache, and need.

When we come to Jesus for what He can do, He will not entrust Himself to us, and we will miss the fullness of who He is.

Did you know that Jesus wants to entrust Himself to you?

My prayer for you through this book is that you would never be fully satisfied by the stories. My prayer is that my experiences would awaken in you a hunger, a longing, and a deep desire to know Him better.

Jesus has things He wants to say to *you*, things that He won't tell me or your pastor or anyone else. He has words to reveal that are for your ears only, unless He asks you to share them with someone else.

Please don't ever make the mistake of parking under one author or teacher and vicariously relating to the Lord through them. Don't rob yourself of the joy, the thrill, or the peace that only He can give when you come to Him for Him.

Not for miracles. Not for health. Not for increase or wisdom or knowledge, though it may please Him to give you those things.

Make knowing Him the highest priority in your life, let nothing keep you from a daily diet of His Word. Drink deeply from the living water. Draw close to Him, then closer still.

I leave you with the words of Paul:

> But whatever things were gain to me, those things I have counted as loss for the sake of Christ. More than that, I count all things to be loss in view of the surpassing value of knowing Christ Jesus my Lord, for whom I have suffered the loss of all things, and count them but rubbish so that I may gain Christ.
>
> —Philippians 3:7-8 NASB